Published on the occasion of the State Visit to the United Kingdom of

Carlo Azeglio Ciampi

President of the Republic of Italy

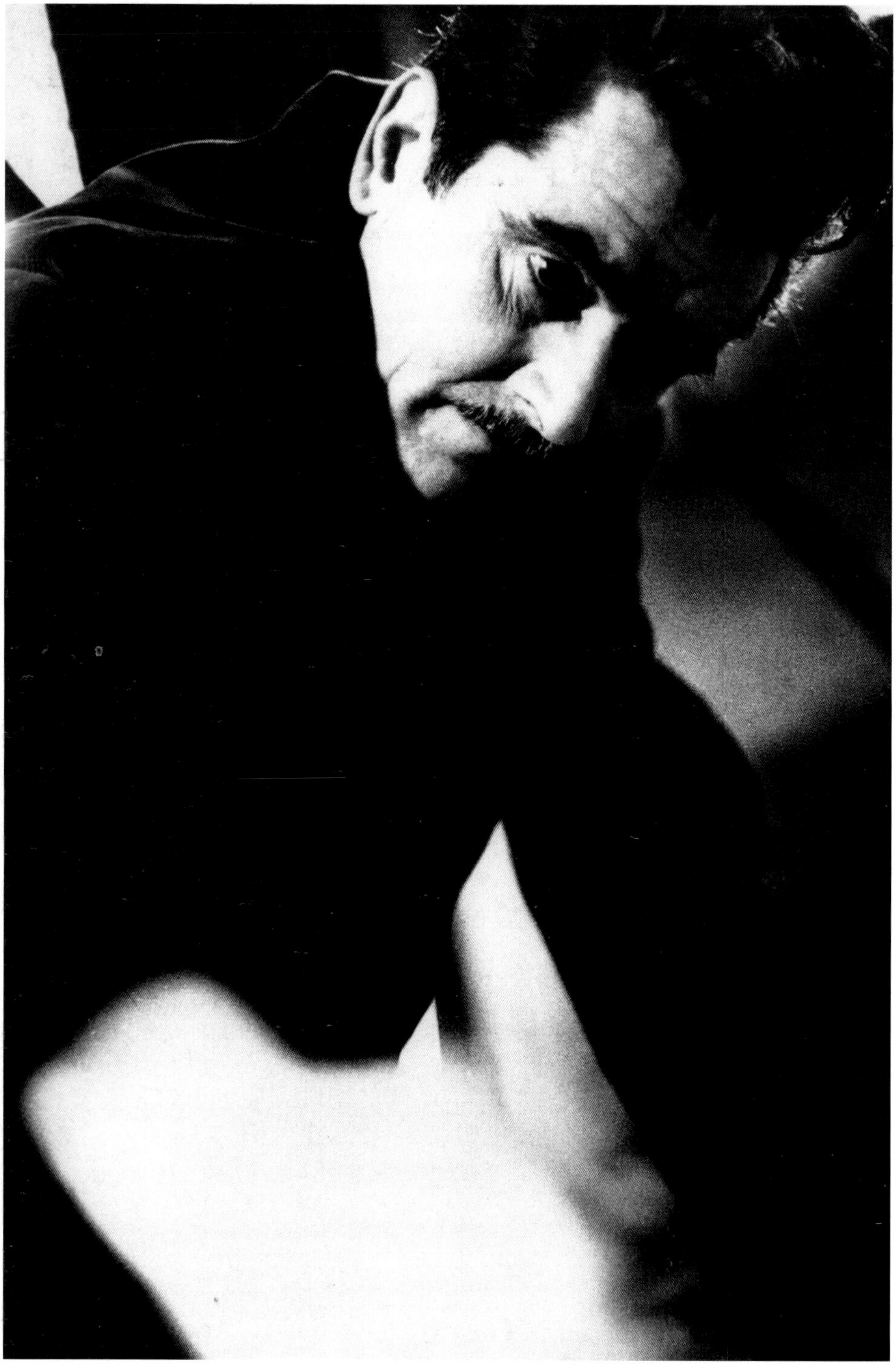

Alberto Burri, 1954

BEYOND PAINTING
BURRI FONTANA MANZONI

Matthew Gale and Renato Miracco

Tate Publishing
in association with
Mazzotta

First published 2005 by order of the Tate Trustees
by Tate Publishing, a division of Tate Enterprises Ltd,
Millbank, London SW1P 4RG
www.tate.org.uk/publishing

On the occasion of the exhibition
Beyond Painting: Burri, Fontana, Manzoni
at Tate Modern
12 March 2005 – 28 February 2006

Supported by the Italian Ministry of Foreign Affairs,
the Italian Embassy, and the Italian Cultural Institute, London

Front cover (from left)
Alberto Burri, *Sacking and Red*, 1954 (detail), Tate, London
Lucio Fontana, *Spatial Concept 'Waiting'*, 1960 (detail), Tate, London
Piero Manzoni, *Achrome*, 1958 (detail), Tate, London

Page 2
Federico Patellani, *Alberto Burri in 1954*; courtesy Archivio Patellani, Milan

Photograph Credits
Corrado De Grazia, Rome: pp. 53-54
Tate, London: pp. 16, 37, 71, 93, 105, 111, 127
Paolo Vandrasch, Milan: p. 59

Printed in Italy by Arti Grafiche Salea, Milan
Bound in Italy by Lego Service, Milan

British Library Cataloguing in Publication Data
A catalogue record for this book is available from the British Library

Library of Congress Cataloguing in Publication Data
Library of Congress Control Number: 2005922313

ISBN 1 85437 614 4

Contents

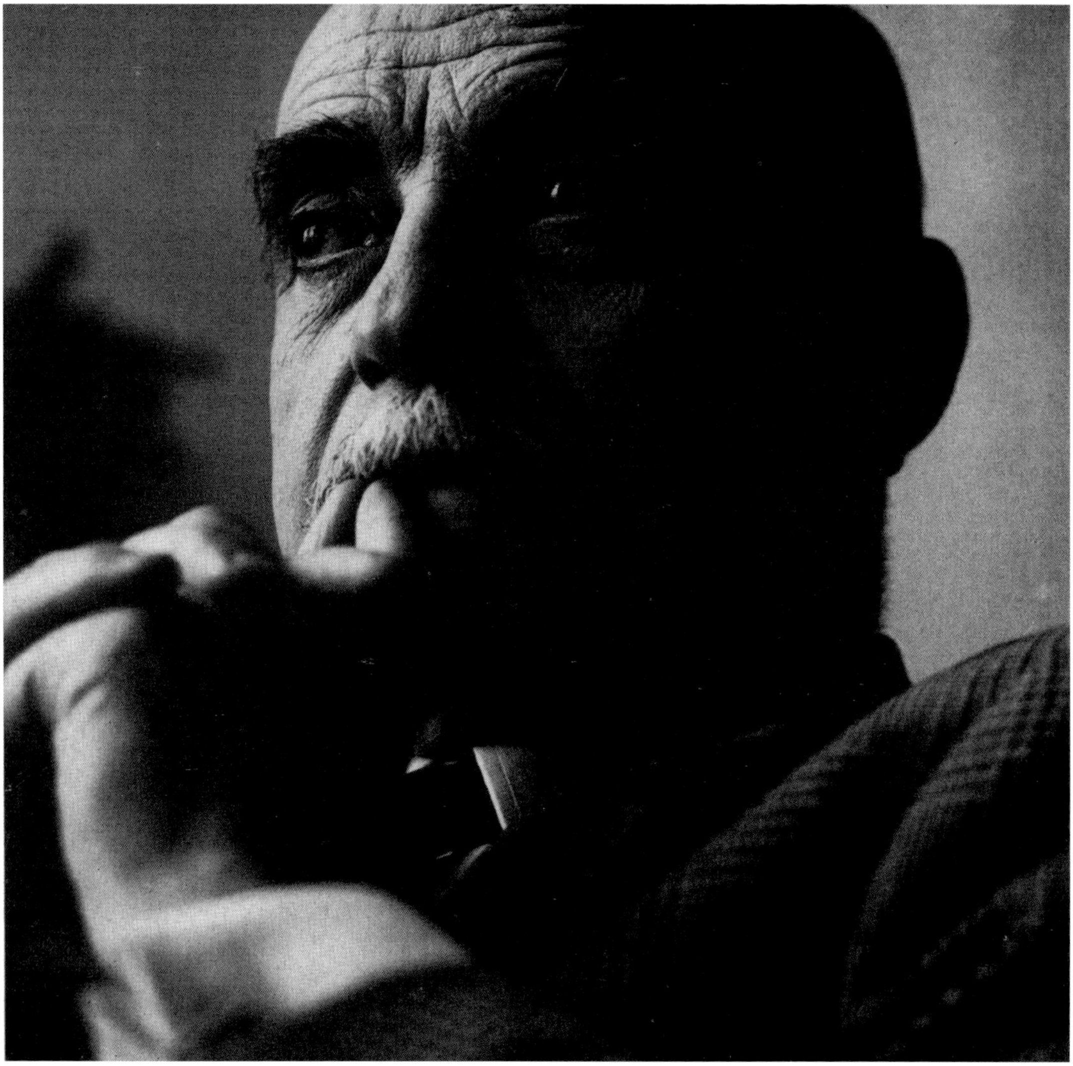

Lucio Fontana, c. 1960

Preface

Italian artistic developments within the cultural scene of the 1950s undoubtedly form a basis for the subsequent pictorial evolution in Europe and America, as well as in Italy. A thematic variety, from the material to *Spazialismo*, characterises the cultural fertility that, today more than ever, can be raised to an international level, showing Italian art to be more that a history of isolated individuals but rather to be active on a more interconnected and complex front.

It is a great honour to present, in the context of the State Visit to the United Kingdom of President Carlo Azeglio Ciampi, an exhibition concentrated upon those years and three such figures as Alberto Burri, Lucio Fontana and Piero Manzoni.

This exhibition represents a notable event for the Italian Ministry of Foreign Affairs as a collaboration with Tate Modern, one of the most prestigeous galleries of modern art in the world, whom we have helped to realise this project. It is particularly gratifying to know that the exhibition, which is unprecedented in Britain, will last a year and thus reinforce cultural foundations on which so many other bilateral initiatives can be built.

The event, made possible thanks to the collaboration of the Fondazione Burri, the Fondazione Fontana and the Archivio Manzoni who have lent major works by each of the artists, offers a window onto a period of Italian art which remains little known abroad. I offer my sincere congratulations to the Presidents of these foundations, to the Director of Tate Modern, to the Ambassador, to the Curators of the exhibition and all those who have collaborated on this initiative.

Gianfranco Fini
Italian Minister of Foreign Affairs

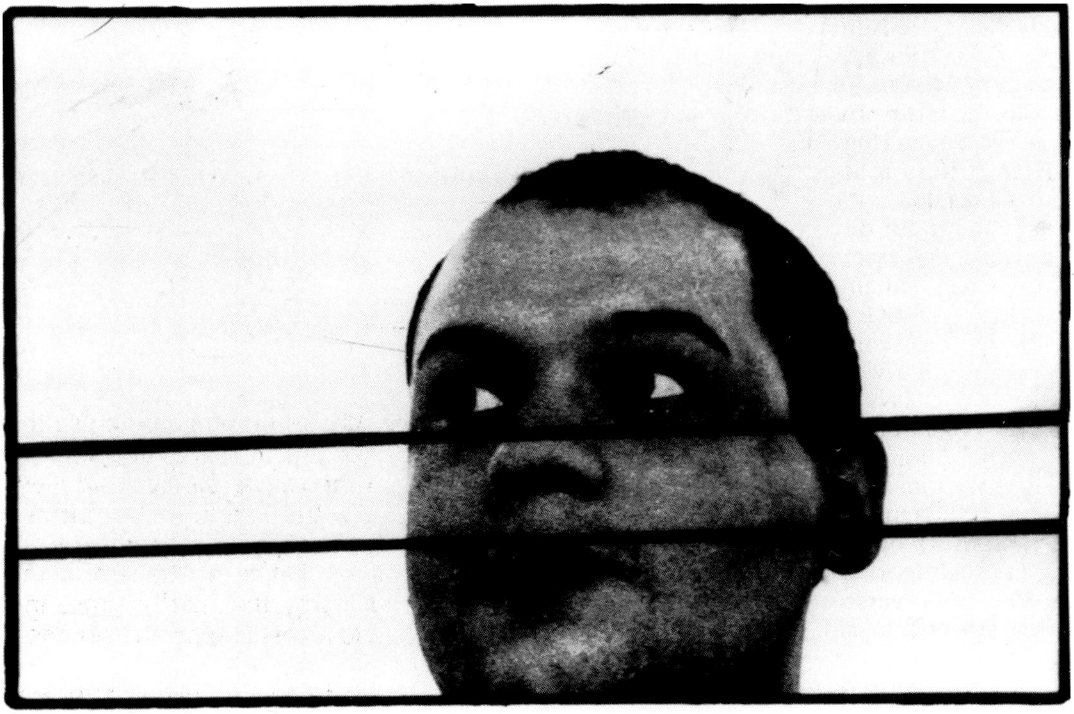

Piero Manzoni, c. 1960

Foreword

It is around half a century since Alberto Burri began to use the discarded sacking of post-war reconstruction as a raw material, and since Lucio Fontana pierced the canvas surface and Piero Manzoni adopted kaolin as a neutral medium. Their move *beyond painting* came at a moment of remarkable experimentation during which they helped to transform the cultural scene of the 1950s in a way that had a profound impact within and beyond Italy, and across Europe and America.

More than that, Burri, Fontana and Manzoni were prominent among the artists who redefined what it has meant to make art in the last fifty years. They used unorthodox materials for revolutionary times, laying new demands on the viewers' expectations. As if aware of the fragility of what had been secured by 1955, Burri expounded a personal credo: 'I can only say this: painting for me is a freedom attained, constantly consolidated, vigilantly guarded so as to draw from it the power to paint more.' Manzoni, the youngest of these artists, claimed a freedom to experiment, asserting: 'in order to leave the earth one must have wings.' Their art embodied release and exploration, which significantly altered the way in which artists subsequently worked around the world.

At the time, each of these artists was received with consternation and fascination. Burri's *sacchi* (sacking pieces) were refused when submitted for the Venice Biennale of 1952, and Fontana actively protested when *Spazialismo* was overlooked by the same exhibition four years later. However, their works were widely seen in Italy and abroad with increasing impact during the second half of the 1950s. While the decade closed with solo exhibitions in London, their work only gradually entered the Tate collection, with the acquisition of major early Fontanas and our important, but solitary, Burri. Manzoni followed after the monographic exhibition at Tate in 1973. By that time, each in his way was associated with the emergence of the next generation of *Arte Povera* artists, whose political and material reflection upon the post-war rejuvenation of Europe – however much it marked a departure – was viewed as indebted to their guiding principles. As one might expect, their relative fortunes in Britain have differed somewhat. Both Fontana and Manzoni have been the subject of substantial exhibitions in recent years (at the Hayward and the Serpentine galleries respectively), but Burri has suffered rather from neglect. The present selection of his works, although by no means on a comparable scale, is a step towards redressing this situation.

The genesis for the present project lies in the fruitful exchanges that came out of the two Tate Modern exhibitions of 2001: *Arte Povera* (organised with the Walker Art Center, Minneapolis) and *Giorgio Morandi*. The collector Isabella del Frate Rayburn spoke passionately about Burri with Frances Morris and Matthew Gale (who, respectively, co-curated these exhibitions), and together they visited the collection that he had gathered in his hometown of Città di Castello. The extraordinary versatility and ambition of his work is evident in the permanent installation that he made there in the Palazzo Albizzini and this convinced the curators that it should be better known to a wider public in Britain.

Three and a half years later, the result is to bring Burri's work to Tate Modern in conjunction with choice works by Fontana and Manzoni, two of his most innovative contemporaries. Although taking the form of a small exhibition, the selection will be displayed for an extended period and is rooted in Tate's own collection. It offers a view onto a crucial moment in recent cultural practice, rather than attempting a comprehensive overview of the period or a survey of each of the artists' output. The selection has been made by Matthew Gale, Tate Curator, and guest curator Renato Miracco. They have focused to the period 1950–63 (the end-date marked by Manzoni's premature death) in order to seize the most innovative exploration of materiality that each artist brought, in highly individual ways, to the shift beyond painting. This is evident, above all, in the physical encounter with the work. It is also brought out in this accompanying catalogue, in which Renato Miracco provides an overview of the trajectory towards the fertility of that moment, while Matthew Gale, stimulated by the artists' own publications, offers an alphabet of appropriate fragments.

This project would not have been possible without the generosity and help of colleagues and friends in Italy. I should like to add to the curator's acknowledgements my own thanks to the artists' foundations and all those, named and anonymous, who have lent and advised. We are honoured that President Ciampi should have agreed to be patron of the exhibition. All aspects of our desire to bring these works to Britain were facilitated by the President's interest and the crucial assistance offered by Gianfranco Fini, Italian Minister of Foreign Affairs. This was, at all times, augmented by the enthusiastic collaboration of His Excellency Ambassador Giancarlo Aragona and his staff at the Italian Embassy in London as well as their colleagues at the Italian Cultural Institute. We are most grateful for all their efforts, without which the idea may well have remained an ideal.

Vicente Todolí
Director, Tate Modern

Curators' Acknowledgements

In a catalogue of self-characterisations through which he tried to answer whether he was really 'an Italian', the author Ennio Flaiano wrote: 'I like to travel in Italy and almost every place in it enchants me and makes me want to stay here. Seen in this light I could very well be an Englishman.' While this is a wry reflection on stereotypes, Flaiano's view also captures the Forsterian love of Italy so often attributed to the British. It was just such a rose-tinted view that the Futurists had sought to dispel at the beginning of the twentieth century, but by the 1950s a new confidence appeared to throw-off this historical yolk.

Tate has a longstanding interest in Italian art and this particular project (as noted in the Director's Foreword) goes back to the successes of the *Arte Povera* and *Giorgio Morandi* exhibitions of 2001. The collector Isabella del Frate Rayburn subsequently urged a visit to the Fondazione Burri in Città di Castello where the multifaceted inventiveness of Burri's activities is conveyed in astonishing strength by the choice holding which he himself collected and displayed in the Palazzo Albizzini. We are indebted to the knowledge, expertise and generous hospitality of all at the Fondazione, especially Maurizio Calvesi, Nemo Sarteanesi and Chiara Sarteanesi. Although Burri's display of his own works at the Palazzo is immovable, the rich holdings of the Fondazione's collection have ensured that really extraordinary pieces can be seen for an extended period at Tate Modern. This makes it especially saddening that the artist's widow, Minsa Burri, did not live to see this resolution of our project.

While there are many merits in seeing an artist's work in isolation, from an early stage we believed that a conjunction of Burri's work with that of his contemporaries, Lucio Fontana and Piero Manzoni, would be enormously enriching. The small selection of important works affords an opening onto the vibrant development of art in Italy in the 1950s. Fontana was the oldest of the three and his influence was pervasive during the period when he was first acknowledged as one of the most innovative international figures. Manzoni was more than thirty years younger, and while his practices in many ways extend the vocabulary of the older artists, they may also be seen as a salutary critique. The result of this conjunction is a small but powerful group of mutually enriching works that speak for a period of enormous fertility.

The exhibition has benefited from the enthusiasm of the Italian Minister of Foreign Affairs Gianfranco Fini and of His Excellency Ambassador Giancarlo Aragona. In Rome, we have had the continual support of the Ministry of Foreign Affairs' Cultural Promotion and Cooperation Department, notably Director General Anna Blefari-Melazzi, Deputy Director General Lucio Alberto Savoia, Head of Office II (Cultural Events) Mauro Marsili and Anna Elisa Zaffi; and at the Ministry of Culture we had the continual support of the Direzione Generale per l'Architettura e l'Arte Contemporanea (DARC), notably Director General Pio Baldi, Anna Martirolo and Stefania Vannini. In London, we have benefitted from the support of the Italian Cultural Institute, notably Director Pierluigi Barrotta and Deputy Director Giovanna Gruber, as well as Cultural and Press attaché Agostino Palese and his colleagues at the Embassy. Their dedication to the project has been energising and their collaboration on all aspects unstinting.

The successful resolution of this project is, as ever, the result of the goodwill and advice of many people. The initial idea came from conversations with Isabella del Frate Rayburn and Frances Morris and has been developed in detail through energetic visits and debates. Whatever the intent, such a project can only become actual through the generosity of the lenders. For their loans over an unusually long period, we are extremely grateful to the following: President Professore Maurizio Calvesi, the General Secretary Nemo Sarteanesi and the curator Chiara Sarteanesi of the Fondazione Palazzo Albizzini 'Collezione Burri' in Città di Castello; Nini Ardemagni Laurini, President of the Fondazione Lucio Fontana in Milan; Professoressa Elena Manzoni di Chiosca and Rosalia Pasqualino di Marino of the Archivio Piero Manzoni, Milan. We have also benefited from the generosity of various private collectors who have agreed to lend: Isabella del Frate Rayburn, Silvia and Angelo Calmarini, and others who prefer to remain anonymous.

As well as the lenders and the Foundations, who have provided important insights into the artists' works, the substance of this catalogue rests – as any work on the period must – on the scholarship of a group of writers. We should single out Guido

Ballo, Maurizio Calvesi, Germano Celant, Enrico Crispolti, and Jole de Sanna among many to whom our texts are indebted. In other capacities we would like to thank Attilio Codognato, Roberto and Paola Giovanelli, Biancamaria Giuganino Parkin, Rowena Fuller, and others who have helped along the way.

At all stages the project has benefited from the advice at Tate of Vicente Todolí, whose support for the idea has been crucial. Frances Morris, who has been a sounding board along the way, and Nicholas Serota, Jan Debbaut and Sheena Wagstaff have all offered crucial advice. Colleagues in a wide variety of functions across Tate have brought their customary combination of calm, professionalism and imagination to the project. We would especially thank: Kia Hing Fay and Jules Breeze among the Registrars; Jacqueline Hill, Head of Tate Legal and Melissa Bolton; Jennifer Cormack, Suzanne Freeman and Brad MacDonald in Development and Events; Conservators Patricia Smithen and Elizabeth MacDonald; Marcus Leith in Photography; Kersten Knepper, Rachel Fleming Mulford, Rebecca Lancaster, Paul MacAree at Tate Modern; Phil Monk and the Art Handling team; Simon Bolitho, Jane Burton and Dominic Willsdon in Interpretation; Ruth Finlay, Caroline Priest and Emma Clifton in Press and Communications. Lucy Askew and Giorgia Bottinelli, in Tate Collection, have each helped enormously.

This catalogue has been seen to resolution at Tate Publishing under the watchful eyes of Judith Severne, editor, and Roger Thorp, Publishing Director; Michela Parkin, who made the translation from Italian, Alessandra Serri and Emma Woodiwis provided help at vital moments. It has been produced in association with Edizioni Gabriele Mazzotta in Milan, where the welcome has combined great warmth and a fertility of ideas at all stages. We would like to thank Gabriele Mazzotta, Bianca Mazzotta and Martina Mazzotta, as well as Roberta Riotti, for her design, and Monica Maroni, for her editorial work, and their colleagues for transforming the sketch of an idea into a handsome publication available both in English and Italian.

The great challenge of a project such as this is to retain the charge of excitement and to find ways of conveying it to a wider audience. All these people, and more, have helped to make this possible. The extraordinary inventiveness of the three artists has made it rewarding.

Matthew Gale and *Renato Miracco*

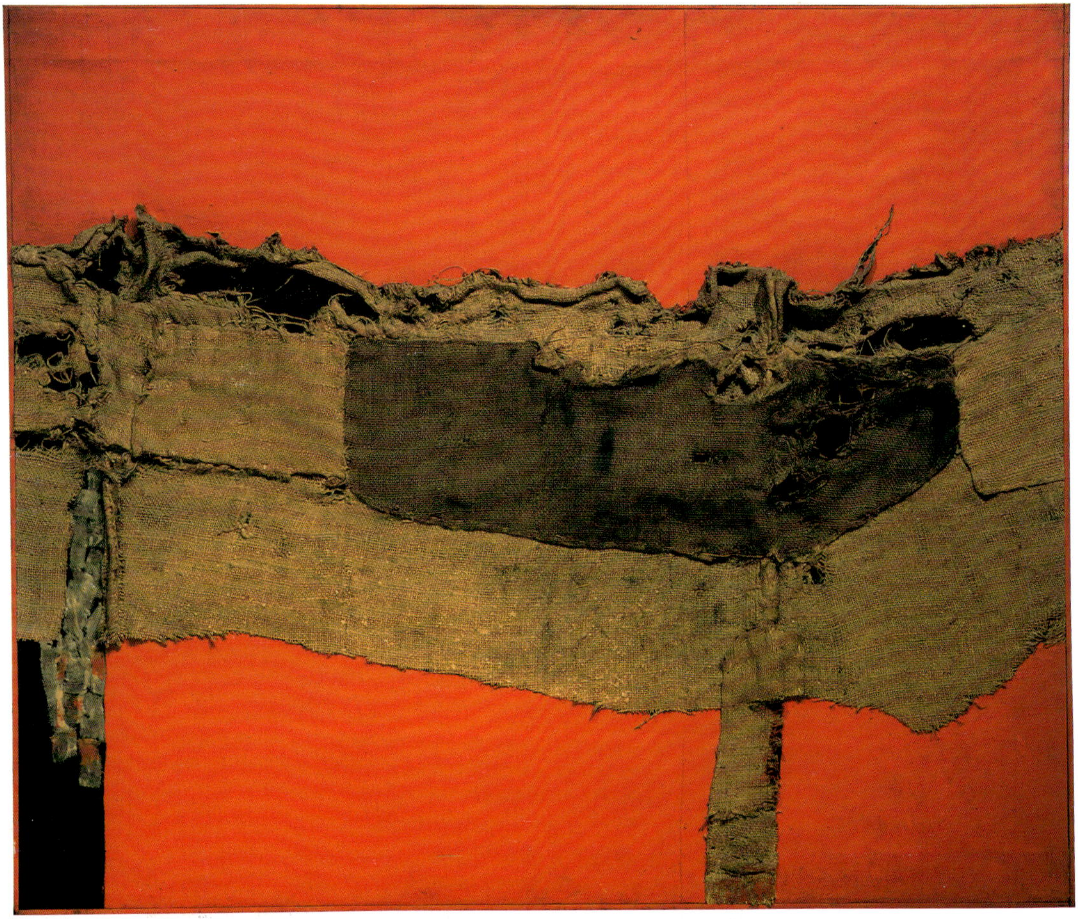

Alberto Burri
Sacco e rosso, 1954, *Sacking and Red*
Sacking and oil on canvas, 86.4 × 100.3 cm
Catalogo sistematico: 239 (see p. 135)
Tate, London

Encounters with Matter

Renato Miracco

> That which is created is nothing but a bridge between the external plastic infinity and the internal plastic infinity ... We Futurists insist that even twenty different types of materials can be used in a single work of art in order to achieve plastic movement. To mention a few examples: glass, wood, card, iron, cement, horse-hair, leather, cloth, mirror, electric lights.
> (Umberto Boccioni, *Manifesto tecnico della scultura futurista*, Milan, 11 April 1912)

The Italian exploration of the valency of matter began in earnest in the first half of the twentieth century. Matter began to be seen not as a static decorative element but as a dynamic organic entity resulting in that unique object which is neither painting nor sculpture. Just as in the latter half of 1912, Pablo Picasso instigated parallel experiments in France by introducing found materials into his paintings, so it was also in that year, that Umberto Boccioni began to put his own theories into practice with his *Manifesto tecnico della scultura futurista* (Technical manifesto of Futurist sculpture). In the introduction to the catalogue of the *Première Exposition de Sculpture Futuriste* (First exhibition of Futurist sculpture) he stated:

> I therefore thought that by breaking down the unit of matter into several different materials and using each one of these to characterise a different weight or a different degree of molecular expansion, it would be possible to achieve a dynamic element. The problem of dynamism in sculpture, however, depends not so much on the use of different materials as on the interpretation of form.[1]

In 1914 Boccioni wrote to a friend whom he had commissioned to find materials with which to construct a Futurist sculpture: 'I recommend that you choose the most up-to-date materials you can find, the most rhythmic, the most dynamic, the most battered, ugly, disgusting.'[2] The thinking behind this statement was that the 'emotion of use' within the materials should be transferred to the work of art, as in fact happens in his works

Fusione di una testa e di una finestra (Fusion of a head and a window) and *Testa + casa + luce* (Head + house + light) of 1912. Similarly, Filippo Tommaso Marinetti wrote about a 'lyrical obsession with matter' in his *Manifesto tecnico della letteratura futurista* (Technical manifesto of Futurist literature) of May 1912. Matter was no longer static. In fact, early in the century the British physicist Ernest Rutherford had revealed that matter was dynamic, by bombarding atoms with tiny radioactive particles and thus discovering its inherent energy. This is just one of the many influences that science had upon art and which would lead Marinetti to proclaim:

> The solidity of a strip of steel interests us for itself; that is, the incomprehensible and non-human alliance of its molecules or its electrons that oppose, for instance, the penetration of a howitzer. The warmth of a piece of iron or wood is, in our opinion, more impassioned than the smile or tears of a woman ... We must give the weight and scent of objects.[3]

These artists were at the forefront of developing a new language of art. The new means of understanding found its expression in Giacomo Balla and Fortunato Depero's *complessi plastici* (plastic complexes), proposed in their manifesto *Ricostruzione futurista dell'universo* (Futurist reconstruction of the universe) of 1915. The *complessi plastici* broke with the Boccionian representation of reality that was multi-layered but nevertheless still had its roots in figuration. Instead, they arrived at a completely abstract language, through the use of 'metal wires, cotton, wool, coloured glass, wire mesh, fabrics, mirrors, metallic sheets, coloured foils', or through mechanisms which made the work 'turn' and 'fragment' in its surrounding space, 'mechanical, electronic, musical and noisy gadgets'.[4] This was the point at which, according to Marinetti, art ceased to be the 'memory and burdened re-evocation of a lost object' in order to become 'Art-Action, namely desire, aggression, possession, joy, harsh reality, the geometric splendour of forces, forward-moving'.[5]

The later exploration of – indeed *adventure* into – matter that took place in Italian art cannot be fully understood without a knowledge of such early experiments into its main themes. In looking at Burri, Fontana and Manzoni it is possible to grasp from their own statements that the heritage of their exploration of matter was Futurist, in the broadest sense of the term; their assertions marked a border between what went before and what followed.

The adoption of collage was also, alongside the challenge posed by the *complessi plastici*, responsible for opening up a more systematic and productive field of inquiry into what matter consisted of and how it could constitute a work of art. It is worth noting here particular points along this journey, in order to understand more fully Burri's series of works, Fontana's obsession with the *concetti spaziali*, or Manzoni's white *achromes* (e.g. pp. 16, 37). Alongside artists such as Balla, Mario Sironi, Carlo Carrà, Ardengo Soffici, Gino Severini and Farfa, who used a variety of materials in their paintings (at times substituting them for paint itself in the true spirit of Futurism),[6] or the assemblages of found-objects made by artists such as Gerardo Dottori and Bot, stands the figure of Enrico Prampolini, whose work is the thread that runs through this inquiry into the concept of matter.

> To become matter: the concept of metamorphosis underlies the creation of the elements in a composition in a conceptual process of spiritual transfiguration and formal transposition.
> (Enrico Prampolini, *Arte polimaterica*, 1944)

While a change in the *use* of materials – in the broadest sense – was going on between 1910 and 1960 it is necessary to bear in mind that the very concept of matter also underwent constant change. The renewed attention of art historians and, consequently, of audiences necessitates a shift in the interpretative codes that must be continually adapted to the specific context in which the work of art is made. An appreciation of the work of Burri, Fontana and Manzoni frequently demands a technical and semantic expertise that contradicts any notion of a clearly defined ideology of art. The creation of art in order to perfect on nature, the aesthetic of form as a dialogue between *eidos* (imperceptible form) and *morphe* (perceptible form), art as interpretative understanding, the notion that aesthetics consists of reading iconography and symbolism: all these are concepts that must be repeatedly deconstructed in order to make space for continually evolving terminologies that frequently challenge the status quo, being rich in new aesthetic impulses and novel areas of awareness. Difficulties arise if any attempt is made to impose a fictitious sense of order on the interpretation of phenomena such as Manzoni's *achromes* or his *fiati d'artista* (Artist's breaths), Burri's *Cellotex* (fibre-board) works, or Fontana's *tagli* (cuts). Instead, these works should be accepted as moments of enlightenment unfettered by temporal constraints, within a temporal dialogue that has been freed from the monotony of the everyday.

Manzoni commented: 'I can't understand painters who even now position themselves in front of the canvas as though it were a surface to be covered with colours and forms.'[7] To consider the role of art to be a simple presentation of facts, learnt symbols and reassuring certainties, is to relegate it to a sphere governed by boring and meaningless theories. And it is just this that we should avoid. The language of art has changed and will continue to change. It alters from one artist to another. Artists have assumed the role of shaman, leading us into parallel universes, teaching us a new language each time. It is difficult to employ the same terms to discuss the use of matter in relation to the work of Boccioni, Prampolini, Burri, Fontana, Manzoni, Castellani and Kounellis; this would be like talking merely about oil, watercolour and tempera in discussing artists such as Leonardo, Caravaggio, Duchamp or Rauschenberg. What is more, when we explore the nature of matter, we are not talking about a technique, but about the use of something substantial which is applied, distressed, etched into, slashed, fossilised, even vaporised, in order to become in the end the work of art, that moment of intelligence and intuition which is the artist's gift to us.

The tactile quality of matter (had space allowed, Marinetti's manifesto *Il Tattilismo* (Tactilism) would have been discussed here),[8] and the use and manipulation of matter, each assume a meaning of their own which we shall attempt to reveal, lending the term an almost spiritual meaning. We shall also try to define a conceptualisation of space, of the void, and of time that, in the work of such artists as Fontana, is more to do with a state of flux than with any underlying structure.

Prampolini was the first Italian artist to question the difference between the *use of* material and *being in* matter. Whereas Boccioni used material as a means of building up a sculpture or a painting, for Prampolini in such works as *Béguinage* 1914 or *Stato d'animo marino* (Marine state of mind) 1941, matter was an object in itself. It was a fragment of a past and present life, rendered rich and evocative either through its own material qualities, or through its juxtaposition and relationship with other materials. From this juxtaposition arose a revelation of various sorts, equal to the 'the flashes of inspiration of "ordinary things" ... [that, when they] illuminate art, create these elements which are most essential to our everyday reality'.[9]

What we see – or glimpse – is a vision of a parallel world, a world that comes to be described in terms of the fourth dimension. It is defined, in essence, by different types of matter, by their intrinsic qualities and the relationship established between them. These *polimaterici* (polymaterials) became known as *interviste con la materia* ('encounters with matter' or, literally, 'interviews with matter', terms coined by Prampolini). In 1944 he wrote: 'Encounters with matter were not about a battle against painting, but about taking to its extreme the idea of substituting completely and fundamentally the *reality of paint* with the *reality of matter*.'[10] This explicit difference, which forms the basis for a coherent revisionist dialogue between artist and viewer, allows the viewer to distinguish completely a painted reality from a material reality, so that both can co-exist. The work of art is thus no longer confined arbitrarily within a pictorially defined dimension, but is able to extend towards a reality that can *also* be founded on matter.

'Polymaterial art is not a technique but a rudimentary means of artistic expression', Prampolini stated, 'the evocative power of which resides in the formal arrangement of matter ... *Matter* being something inherent within the natural world (a living organism, consisting of atoms in perpetual motion) as well as having formal transcendence.'[11] In line with these beliefs, he also stated explicitly his desire to 'escape from painting into an aesthetic and technical world in which it is possible to give shape to the human circumstances of the new mystical spirituality in which we live ... Matter can be made spiritual and harmoniously arranged over surfaces in space, where the lively and direct juxtaposition of different materials raises to a higher level the human vision of our era'.[12]

Another important distinction that Prampolini made was the differentiation between *object-matter*, ranging 'from the most base and varied (near-relic of life), to the most refined and worked (whether by hand or machine), and *organic-matter*, whose principle characteristics tend towards an expression of continuity within discontinuity, and of the harmony and dissonance of relationships. These relationships, played out within this dialectic, are not so exclusively relevant to the forms of the object-element, as to the organic existence of matter itself.[13]

This paradigm of oppositions paved the way for a concept of time-based experience that lay at the heart of Fontana's *Manifiesto blanco* (White manifesto), written just two years later, in 1946. On this same subject, Prampolini also wrote about the mnemonic potential of nature, the 'evocative value is in inverse proportion to its visible outward appearance, because it operates in the irrational areas of the spirit; this is how the phenomena of wonder, surprise and the spectacle of miracles are created. Out of this magic worked by matter, in its bio-plastic manifestations, is born the new incantation of polymaterial art'.[14]

All of this was written barely a year before Burri returned to Rome after his experiences as a prisoner-of-war in America. The 'new material code' in Italian art had its own deeply established roots in a novel artistic language, according to which, any intervention into and dialogue with matter required a study of its potential to communicate and its 'feeling for expression', to use a phrase current at the time.

> And America is no longer America, no longer the new world: it is the whole world!
> (Elio Vittorini, *Americana*, Milan 1941)

In the early 1950s, at least until 1952, artistic attention in Italy was very much focused on America and American art, to which the Italians brought their own characteristic energy and desire for mutual exchange, together with a typically Italian multi-layered and complex cultural baggage. However, the beginning of the 1950s also saw the cultural climate in Italy undergo what could be described as a period of 'constructive self-examination', after the thirst for renewal which characterised the immediate post-war period. Artists were caught up in the historical circumstance of their time and forced to confront the unimaginable, armed only with fragmentary ideologies and personal mythologies. Thus the surface of the picture – the work – became the arena, and at times the filter, for the struggle between the emptiness of the imitative image and the urgency with which a 'material other' sought to find its expression. Out of the chaos, canvas and material became privileged places where artists sought to create a fresh taxonomy based in the everyday, but which still permitted a degree of metaphysical experience essential to the creation of a work of art.

This dialectic between universal and individual, between the need for expression and the spiritual condition, between inorganic matter and optical illusion was deeply rooted in a conflict between art itself and the need to bypass form. The desire to transcend form could be seen as a yearning for a spirituality that dematerialises while still remaining inextricably linked to the *res* (the object) and to matter. The resulting images, whether abstract or figurative, visible or invisible, should not be seen simply as representations of an original object which no longer exists, but as evocations, a door through which otherness enters the world of the senses and the work of art becomes a *living form*.

It is through this lens that a view may be taken of attempts by Italian artists, on the one hand, to discover an essential space and, on the other by American artists to unearth a heritage against which they could compare and measure and, ultimately, transform themselves.

Artists such as Fontana, Burri, Antoni Tàpies, Jackson Pollock, Willem De Kooning and Jean Fautrier each discovered on and 'within' the canvas their own dimension, challenged and marked by experience, intimately linked to their own personal identity. The artist commits an act of sacrifice on the surface of the picture, revealing his inner self. At this time, and especially in some of the work produced between 1946 and 1957, a physical relationship with the work of art can be perceived that is almost sensual (for Fontana as much as for Burri, De Kooning, Pollock). This is the need for self-expression within the constant dialectic of everyday constraints. Broadly speaking, from 1950 onwards there exist two main currents or oppositions within art. On the one side, under the generally accepted umbrella of 'Action Painting', stand the artists mentioned above, together with Yves Klein, whose goal was to re-establish action as of paramount importance within painting. On the other side are the adherents of what has been termed 'Logic Painting', who stressed the need for a rational approach, a means of controlling the artistic process by *logic*.[15] It is within these two extremes that the artists of the 1960s operated, making frequent reference to the historical avant-gardes of Dada and Futurism. These years were also characterised by a desire to encapsulate within a single doctrine or approach, a science of pictorial practice that, however, had already shown its limits in the dichotomy of art versus life. The only outsider was doubtless Marcel Duchamp whose practice went beyond art to enter directly into life. What singled him out was his desire to express his artistic self without having to reveal any fundamental truths or overarching social messages. He stands, in fact, as one of the main points of reference for Manzoni.

Travelling back a little, to a consideration of Italy, the bulk of artistic activity took place in Venice, Milan and Rome. Venice, with its Biennales, was the jewel in the crown on an international level. Milan was more progressive and the place where the most cutting-edge movements of the time took shape, home to the *Primo manifesto dello spazialismo* (First manifesto of *Spazialismo*) of 1947 and the *Manifesto della pittura nucleare* (Manifesto of nuclear painting) of 1952. And what of Rome? The critic Milton Gendel recalled:

> When I discovered Rome in 1950, it was pleasantly provincial, it was like going to Connecticut or Westchester ... It was very easy getting into the art world. All art scenes at that time, including New York, were small. If you knew just one person, you quickly knew everyone ... Rome was tiny and people were still in the habit of frequenting cafes ...[16]

In this 'tiny' city in January 1951, Giuseppe Capogrossi, Mario Ballocco, Ettore Colla and Alberto Burri (with his *catrami*, tar works) exhibited together at the Fondazione Origine. Thus they became the *Gruppo Origine*, which proclaimed in its manifesto its intention to 're-present itself as a morally more valid starting point for the demands of non-figuration within expression'.[17] The previous year, 1950, had seen the first one-person exhibition of abstract works by Capogrossi, including his first *Superfici* (Surfaces).

The focus on primordial form was one of the constants underlying the explorations and gradual developments of these years. The same is true of the focus on a primordial *matter*, certainly not a 'virgin' matter, but rather one that had lived more than a little, richly imbued with the experiences of an unconscious and unknown infinity. The Fondazione Origine, in its capacity as an 'international centre for archives and documentation for the study and promotion of abstract art' launched the journal *Arti Visive* in July 1952. This was a time of reflection when the emphasis was on the fact that:

> Every civilisation has left an image, whether in word or sign, the mark of its men and of its culture in history. In its cities, its streets, its spectacles, our civilisation offers a new visual world which is that of contemporary art, the language of which man no longer recognises even in its presence.
> ... To our work to create the images of our civilisation, we want to bring these writings whose purpose is exactly to educate modern man about the visual world of his days, about the consciousness of his nature at this time.[18]

Particularly indicative of the links between Italy and America was the exhibition held in Rome in 1953 entitled *Twenty Imaginary Views of the American Scene by Twenty Young Italian Artists*, curated by the American collector Helena Rubinstein. This exhibition highlights the cultural exchange that existed between the two countries at the time, illustrating how the landmarks of American culture were seen through European eyes: Burri exhibited his work *Jazz*, Afro his work *Chicago*, and Mirko (Basaldella, the latter's brother) a sculpture entitled *Los Angeles*. Alberto Moravia wrote a piece which drew attention to 'the burst of Italian artistic energy which in America has become known as "the Post-war Italian Renaissance"'. This was a pleasing term but, as Moravia himself acknowledged, not an altogether accurate one. What, then, was this new Italian Renaissance founded on, what were its strengths and weaknesses? A statement from Moravia's article provides an indication: 'the term "renaissance" is slightly improper as it implies a rebirth, which actually there never was, indeed, there has been nothing of the sudden or extemporaneous in the course of Italian art in recent years.'[19]

Without doubt – and this has already been seen to be the case with the concept of matter – the environment already existed for a resolution of the question of form. Developments had taken place within the direct legacy of Futurism. As the painter Carla Accardi wrote in 1955: 'My goal is simply to depict the vital impulse in the world.'[20] This avant-garde impulse was reaffirmed by the artist Piero Dorazio in 1954 in his article 'New Italian Art: A Promise', in which he outlined developments within Italian art from Futurism to abstraction.

> The impact of the leading art forms among the present generation can be traced to the early 30s when a small group of artists took a fresh look at Futurism, accepted it as their only

> tradition, and attempted to translate into a native idiom the experiences of abstract art and surrealism ...
> Abstract art in Italy still is rather a symbol of renewal for progressive minds than a definite tendency, but it associates all the various contemporary manners and is today certainly the most fertile experimental field.[21]

This push forward by the avant-garde was opposed by 'socialist realism', which had been adopted by the communist parties as the means of expressing within painting the class war on behalf of socialism. It constituted a sort of 'partial account rather than a complete history of Society and contemporary Culture'.[22]

The dialogue between American and Italian art continued with an exhibition held at the Museum of Modern Art, New York, in 1955 entitled *The New Decade: 22 European Painters and Sculptors*, curated by Andrew C. Ritchie. Among the Italian artists invited were the painters Afro, Burri, and Capogrossi, and the sculptors Mirko and Luciano Minguzzi. Dore Ashton reviewed the show for the *New York Times Magazine*:

> Of the two groups the Europeans are more closely linked with the art of their own immediate past, while the Americans, with neither the advantages nor the disadvantages of a busy modern tradition, are inclined to take more risks with fresh ways of seeing and with new techniques. But both insist that their art is based on personal experience of things seen and felt. And in the common pursuit and reinterpretation of art's enduring values there are no national differences.[23]

Two characters provided the focus for the artistic exchange between America and Italy: Burri and Afro, between whom existed a particularly strong relationship of artistic give-and-take.

It should be made plain at this point that both Italian and American efforts were focused on building up and subsequently undermining *symbolic* (to use a slightly inappropriate term) constructions, which are themselves alien to human subjectivity. This symbolic activity in fact leaned heavily towards objectivity. It was a type of art founded on form and the understanding of form. An extreme interpretation of this was articulated by Remo Bianco in 1956 in his *Manifesto dell'Arte Improntale* (*impronta* meaning imprint), when he asserted that 'the art of the future is situated under the banner of the IMPRINT. AN IMPRINT IS ANYTHING WHICH CREATS A LASTING IMPRESSION ON OUR SUBCONSCIOUS '.[24] It so happened that 1956 was also the year in which Manzoni was experimenting with new forms of painting using the imprint of various everyday objects on canvases with plain backgrounds. The idea of the imprint, furthermore, is closely linked to those *traces*, of great totemic value, which are the universal archetypes that would become so important to the work of Manzoni and already lay at the core of Capogrossi's new painting.

> Words are no help to me when I try to speak about my painting. It is an irreducible presence which refuses to be converted into any other form of expression. It is a presence both imminent and active.
> (Alberto Burri, *The New Decade*, exh. cat., Museum of Modern Art, New York 1955)

> The words don't mean anything to me; they talk around the picture. What I have to express appears in the picture.
> (Alberto Burri in Milton Gendel, 'Burri Makes a Picture', *Art News*, 1954)

In 1953 the Fondazione Origine organised a solo exhibition of Burri. Writing in *Arti Visive*, Emilio Villa described the show:

> Burri Alberto cultivates both in vitro and in linen
> Those contractile anatomies of unexpressed organisms
> Waffling between a semblance of useless biological materials
> And an ideal of fulminating universes
> Between the gigantic and the infinitesimal: a
> Gaping ambiguity, a desire to clutch
> Memories of things that have to be clarified[25]

It may seem contrary to analyse Burri when he himself described his work as beyond words. Let us imagine going, then, simply as visitors, not as critics or art historians, to the artist's collection in the Fondazione Albizzini in Città di Castello, and, from the very first room, let us leave behind all our preconceived ideas and prior knowledge and try to understand Burri's language. Let us strip away our notions of nineteenth-century aesthetic categories and set about discerning the continually changing essence of the work. In this way, the history of art becomes simply the reconstruction of an object through whatever code has been predetermined by the artist.

To do so, we have to achieve a 'new degree of contemplation', and give ourselves time to establish a dialogue with the work of art (see p. 29). What is immediately apparent is the dynamism of matter, the tension between the material and the fragility of the viewer's self. This becomes our new point of departure: not a misdirection but a confirmation. On the one hand lies the material, such as sacking, which becomes the visible trace of a person or event. On the other hand is the viewer who, by means of their ready acceptance of this reality, in this 'here and now', expects nothing more than an exchange, both physical and emotional. The picture will seem almost to throb, leaving one terrified and slightly dazed. This first encounter is achieved through steady observation, and is followed by a moment of clarity, a 'wound' or 'opening', a 'key' with which to enter into the work. After this the 'material object', the primordial matter of which the world is made, will be perceived. Each artwork by Burri acts as a filter, a stage set in which the viewer is on this side of the picture and yet is able to make out something on the other side, beyond the material. Aesthetic pleasure is experienced in front of the work, but it is not this that evokes a feeling of sensual enjoyment. Aesthetic pleasure enables understanding, but it is the mental enjoyment derived from an encounter with Burri's work that is uppermost.

This conceptual engagement with the work manifests itself in three ways, each of which allows a different understanding. The first is *poesis*, or the actual making of the work of art, which is linked to the technical knowledge inherent in creating, constructing and planning. The second is *aisthesis*, or learning to perceive the world in a manner that is neither utilitarian nor pragmatic; this knowledge is intuitive in nature and deconstructs the physical world, offering access to a cosmological vision with the potential to form links between its various manifestations. The third is *katharsis*, namely the identification of the self with a character and a sense of shared social values: even this moment contains within it an element of knowledge, which manifests itself in the ability to communicate personal experience.

The way in which the work of art is received is thus both the next step in a process and, at the same time, an essential part of the work itself, much as an historical event cannot be fully understood without knowledge of its consequences. Similarly, a true understanding of Burri's work necessitates knowledge of its subsequent effects. It is here that the role of silence within it becomes important. There is no noise, only a gentle pulsing: the thinnest of veils dividing us from the world stage in which our logic no longer holds sway. On the viewer's side of the picture everything has taken place, the daily grind, wars, struggles, pain. But behind the curtain Burri allows us to glimpse a light, a sense of hope to which we will desperately cling in an agony of anxiety. This is the encounter with a religious sensibility, rarely sought but frequently experienced in art and religion, in which art has renounced any traditional cognitive values and religion has abandoned any aspiration to dogma. By this means one arrives at an aesthetic of experience which involves the entire work of art. This is hard to put into words, just as Burri asserted.

To *poesis*, that is the technical skill of actually making the work of art, Burri on several occasions entrusts his use of different materials whose 'rough appearance is offset by their expressive perfection'. '

There is no programme in my combining of materials because

Alberto Burri
Sacco e oro, 1953, *Sacking and Gold*
Sacking and gold on canvas, 124 × 109.5 cm
Catalogo sistematico: 395 (see p. 135)
Fondazione Palazzo Albizzini 'Collezione Burri', Città di Castello

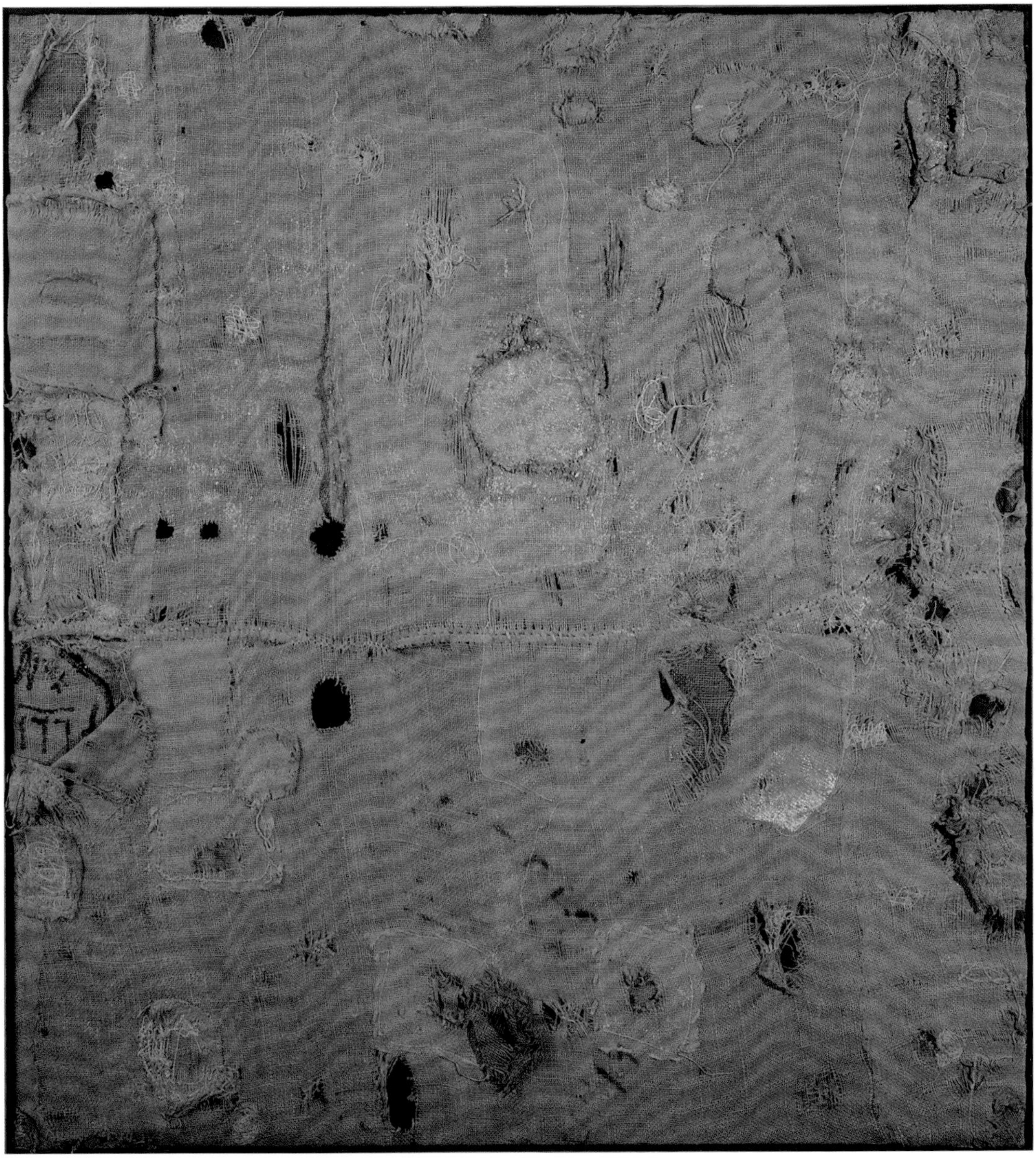

> there is no need for paints, for brushes ... the contribution of the material is minimal. The softness of wood and the hardness of iron are certainly not the principle characteristics of the picture. The principle characteristic is the form.[26]

As much as this statement of Burri's is true, it is also true that the artist arranged for his *sacchi* (sacks), the canvases that he made as a means of pure artistic survival in the concentration camp in Hereford, Texas, to be shipped to Italy via the Red Cross.

> Then I destroyed almost all of them. I only kept four or five, amongst which was the first that I had made, as much to record those beginnings as to demonstrate that, from the outset, mine was work of quality.[27]

Within the broader notion of *poesis*, then, are contained the realities of manual labour, repair, and the straining of seams under pressure, characteristic of patched and reinforced fabrics. On some pieces of sacking imprints of the US flag are partially visible, revealing their original use by the Americans as sacks for sending aid to Europe under the terms of the Marshall Plan. This attention to detail, so often undervalued, is the heritage of a material that is evocative, permeated by history, patience, skill (needle and thread being more important than paint), constructed and repaired, created in its turn by the joining of diverse materials, frequently unravelling, restored to new life.

Thus, using precise and careful gestures in the construction of his picture, the artist is engaged in a cognitive undertaking, a search for the meaning contained within line, light, colour, relief, mass and the tensioning of fabric. This is the case of the *gobbi* (hunchbacks) – where canvas is stretched almost to breaking point so as to suggest indeterminate forms bulging through from behind the picture (p. 99). An intimacy is thus established between the viewer and the viewed. The artist gives visible form to that which is generally accepted to be invisible, and offers a new type of experience in which the viewing process is analogous to the sense of touching and being touched. If it were possible to touch Burri's paintings, the gap between seeing and feeling would be virtually bridged. Here the discussion moves from *poesis* on to *aisthesis*, which, for Burri, is defined largely by beauty.

> I see beauty and that is all. And beauty is beauty and that is all, whether it is a beautiful *sacco* or whether it is a beautiful *legno*, *ferro* or anything else ... I am sure that every picture that I make, whatever the material, is perfect as far as I am concerned. Perfect in form and space. Form and space: these are the essential qualities that really count.[28]

This statement about beauty can be read in the light of the philosophy of Jean-Paul Sartre, for whom the work of art existed at a perpetual remove, being permanently absent. Thus reality can never be beautiful and beauty can never be real. Burri believed that his art could not be described in words. Poetic language and works of art in general are defined precisely by their rejection of the pragmatic and servile language of economics and rational thought. Poetry is therefore freed from the base and scheming intentions of utilitarian existence. Poetry renders nil the things of which it speaks, while allowing us that entry into the collective unknown, that gives rise to 'knowing-feeling': and this is *katharsis*.

Everything in Burri's work should be considered as at the periphery of experience: from his *muffe* (mould works) to his *catrami* (tar pieces), from his *plastiche* (plastic pieces) to his *ferri* (iron works), from his *combustioni* (combustions) to his *Cellotex* (fibreboard) works. Even so, matter contains within itself a sense of history and has undergone change over time. The tar conceals. The fire destroys, leaving behind visible traces; Burri was already experimenting with fire traces on paper in 1953 and 1954, in his illustrations to accompany the poems of Emilio Villa. In his *ferri* (irons), with their tightly welded joints, it is possible to imagine they contain fragments of the ancient armour of the Titans (p. 91). This is one way of reading his work, and, as Villa commented, 'the critics were quick to categorise Burri's work as an inventory, albeit an eccentric and challenging one, of symbols of action: wounding and healing, mutilating and reassembling, cutting and sewing, burning and quenching'.[29] To this list should be added: using and re-using. His use of materials is not in opposition to painting but, in this case, supplants the act of painting itself, the use of the brush. Villa qualified his statement with the assertion that critical activity is, of necessity, after the event and concerned with factual detail; what is more, its deficiencies are exposed by the ability of poetry to penetrate beyond the surface.

If Burri intervenes in the energy of matter, opening up a discussion with a later generation of artists working in the 1960s, such as Jannis Kounellis and Pino Pascali, it is in a different way to Robert Rauschenberg. Despite this, they have been frequently linked in critical writing, since they first met in Rome in 1952. If any parallel does exist between them, it is in relation to their use of materials. Rauschenberg uses cast-offs of an industrialised world in which mass communication assumes the role also of personal information, in which symbols of urban life, such as newspapers and magazines, take over from and become akin to personal souvenirs, such as photographs. Rauschenberg's use of materials is diametrically opposed to the western tradition of composition and to 'painting', even when this notion comprises the use of 'poor' (though still sensual) materials.
The American curator James Johnson Sweeney was the first to

recognise what may be called the 'wonder of reason' in Burri's art. Having included his work in a group show at the Guggenheim Museum in 1954, Sweeney published a perceptive monograph the following year, and organised exhibitions of his work in Pittsburgh and at the Venice Biennale in 1958. His reading of Burri's work is an existentialist and symbolic one:

> Burri transforms rags into a metaphor for bleeding human flesh, breathes fresh life into the inanimate materials which he employs, making them live and bleed; then heals the wounds with the same evocative ability and the same sensibility with which he first inflicted them. What for the Cubists would have been reduced to the partial distillation of a painted composition, to a Merzbild for Schwitters, in Burri's hands becomes a living organism: flesh and blood ... The picture is human flesh; the artist a surgeon.[30]

That the wounds were as much psychological as physical had already been articulated by André Pieyre de Mandiargues, who described Burri as 'the painter of desolation and death, the painter of lower worlds, even of hell itself'.[31] As well as these existentialist and apocalyptic readings, subsequent criticism concentrated on trying to explain the revelatory and enlightening process of Burri's work.[32]

Italian critics seemed only to become aware of Burri as his reputation was already being confirmed within the academic and museum communities. Only then were impassioned texts written about him, by Francesco Arcangeli, and by Giulio Argan, who organised the first retrospective of his work in Brussels in 1959.[33] The first in-depth studies of Burri's work were by Maurizio Calvesi,[34] who concentrated on the structure of the works and on the 'destructive-constructive' gesture, by Enrico Crispolti,[35] and by Cesare Brandi, who produced a thorough monograph in 1962, and who famously highlighted the sense of confusion that is experienced by the viewer in front of one of Burri's works.[36]

Of interest to an in-depth analysis of Burri's art is his use of black and gold. Black, beneath which red can often be glimpsed apparently covered and erased (see p. 67), is the base colour of Burri's work, a colour made up of infinite smudgings and deep shadows. Black is never just itself. More than any other colour it alludes to the concrete yet indefinable construction of form, it is associated with form rather than with expression. Occasionally it is the *relic* of a substance or an image, a trace of pictorial writing that exists precisely because all efforts have been taken to erase it. The resulting image thus becomes a referent, a point of departure in understanding the meaning of the work but, as with the origin of all things, that meaning can only follow the referent. The construction of a picture thus involves the choice of its component parts as well as the selection of particular, and at times discordant, characteristics. These become elements in a code applied to the formal properties of the chosen subject matter. Where in the case of Kurt Schwitters, that code may be identified with the use of collage, in Burri's case it is found in a rough black or reddish fabric.

Another element to consider in Burri's art is his use of light. It may seem odd to speak of luminosity in relation to his works, but the fall of light upon the surface is crucial to the optical perception of the depths from which emanate the sense of intrinsic spaciousness (also found in the works of Fontana). Most frequently this is achieved through the use of gold, resulting in a surface that is reflective at certain points in the composition (p. 29). Burri, as has been seen, spoke often of form and the importance of form, which in itself is described by the meeting of lines. Line, in optical terms, is nothing more than an indication of a boundary and in Burri's work it delimits perspectival space. His lines are broken, reconstituted, twisted, but full of energy. The complex spatial structure created by the meeting of lines and assorted materials enriched by paint and colour, whether this is black, gold or red, constitutes the architecture of the work, the underlying structure whose classical or *para*-classical aspect is purely superficial.

Finally, it is significant that Burri, in his constant state of energetic creativity, found his inspiration in nature. The sand and rocks seen in his photographs of the American desert taken in 1958 during one of his numerous visits to his friend Afro are, for example, a clear inspiration for a number of, often small, works which crystallise within their borders the magic of a parallel world. In many respects, his work presents one of the most coherent attempts within twentieth-century art to overcome the distinction between *eidos* and *morphe*, between 'underlying' and 'surface' form. His was an aesthetic evolution of what Rudolf Arnhem calls the 'notion of shape', by which is intended the primary and most simple process of perception. Perception consists in forming visual concepts: the complete appearance of form never provides information about a single object, but rather about the whole to which it belongs. It is in relation to this notion that Burri's images become *iconic*, since the viewer enters the realms of true art only through form, through the transformation of object into image.

FONTANA

> Making art is one of the manifestations of human intelligence; it is difficult to establish its limits, reasoning and needs. There can be no such thing as spatial painting or sculpture, just a spatial concept of art. The element in space in all its dimensions is the only possible evolution of spatial architecture. There exists an art

Lucio Fontana
Concetto spaziale, 1958, *Spatial Concept*
Pastel on canvas, 163.8 × 120.6 cm
Catalogo generale: 58 G 1 (see p. 135)
Tate, London

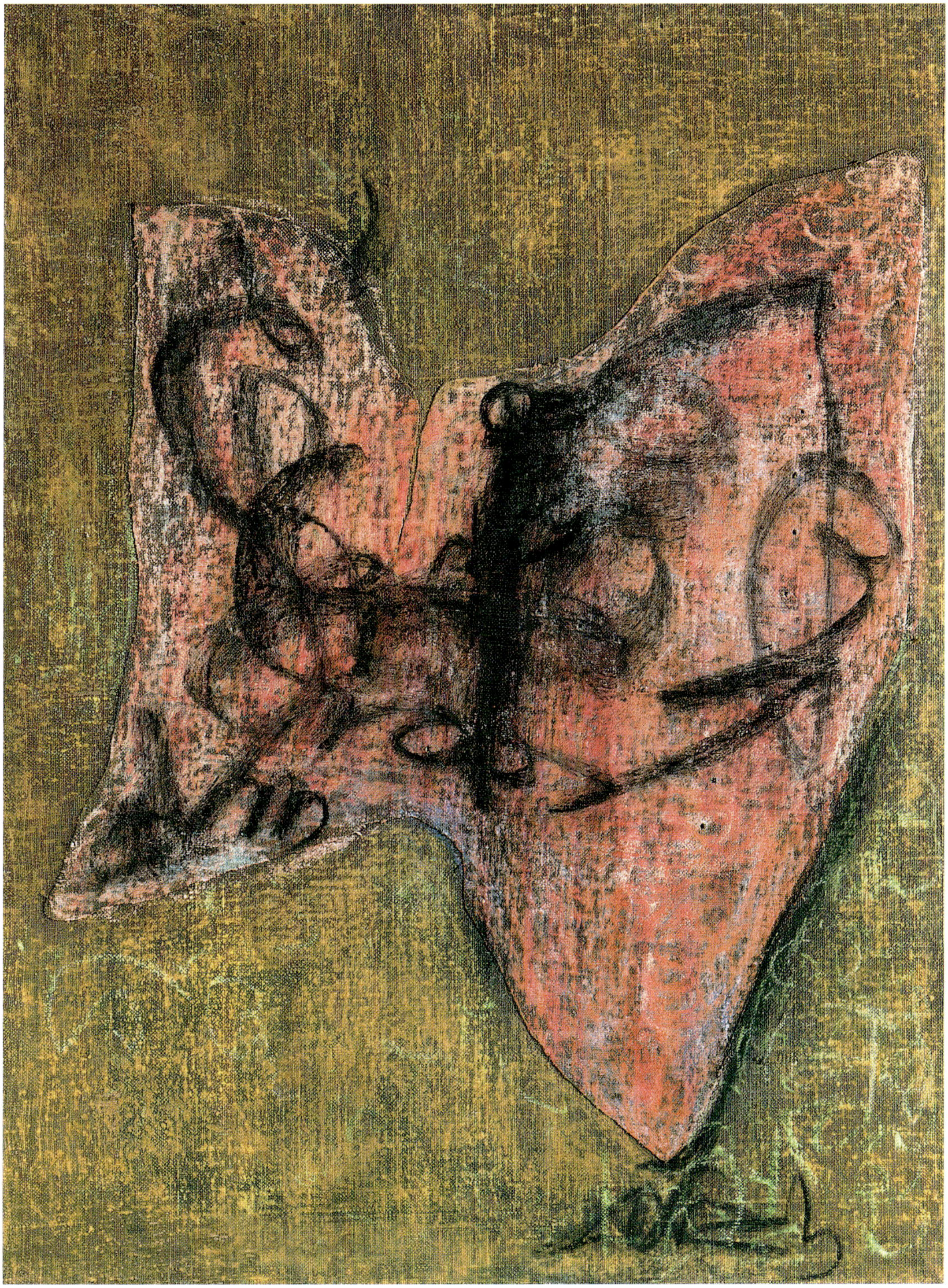

form by 'pouring tar all over him'.[44] This was his first attempt to re-appropriate original substances, without giving in to the requirements of formal aestheticism, in order to arrive at another dimension somewhere between time and timelessness. This was the inception of his idea that a work of art is like a star, whose light travels for a long time before being visible to the observer, and is furthermore characterised by a creative process that seems to secure a dynamic autonomy and independence from the subject. Its intrinsic truth gains eloquence precisely because of the impulse of *res* and *apparition*, defined by Theodor Adorno as thunderbolts. These constitute the sudden appearance within reality of something unexpected and unimaginable, comparable to an explosion the result of which is the reassertion of the spirit – of space – against the imposing power of sensory experience. Within this context the artist is bound to stir up matter, marking it with movement in a synergy which is more than merely gestural. 'It is not true', Fontana remarked, 'that I made holes in the canvas in order to destroy it, no, I made holes in order to discover' and, further still, he continued, to find 'the cosmos of an unknown dimension.'[45] In this case the word 'cosmos' should not be understood in modern terms, where it has become concrete and definable. It should be situated within a notion of incompleteness, of the unfinished, a visible pre-apparition of what should exist but has yet to come into being. Fontana once said: 'I am not interested in the sort of space of which you speak. Mine is another dimension.'[46] Therefore 'there can be no spatial painting or sculpture, only a spatial concept of art';[47] hence the titling of his *Concetti spaziali*.

'If I have made an important discovery, it is without doubt the hole ... The hole was completely outside the dimension of the picture – it conferred the freedom to reconceive art.'[48] Fontana's *buchi* (holes) and *tagli* (cuts) together short-circuited and redefined the infinite within form (see pp. 71, 127). They were the first steps in ensuring that the work, which was neither painting nor sculpture but a singular creation, should become 'dynamic form, through its ever-changing and evolving nature'.[49] These works give off a kind of invisible aura that lies somewhere between object and action, between relative and absolute movement, between the visible and the invisible, between the picture and its cosmic projection. This is where form does not close out the infinite but acts as a channel, a pathway, a flow of free movement. The reference to the Baroque, especially in the works made between 1953 and 1957 (p. 61), is not out of place in this dialogue of contrasts. This is made clear in Umberto Eco's apposite summary, where he speaks of 'that forceful dynamism which, in Fontana's imagination, runs through matter and activates it through its relationship with space'.[50]

Fontana's image acts as pictorial writing, restoring a meaning that is perceived in its totality through the fundamental role of colour and light. Colour, in effect intrinsic to form itself, has a hand in the creation of form and also has an active part in the meaningful substance of the work. It defines the spatial quality. This is also true of light, especially for Fontana's neon sculptures. Light might be arranged as a fixed source or diffuse, with no single precise point on the surface. In the latter case, as in the *buchi* and the *tagli*, it might not appear in keeping with the artist's chosen code. Nevertheless, it is exactly its indeterminate quality that determines the mystery, the cognitive alterity which exists on the other side of the picture-sculpture.

His *tagli* are very different from Burri's cuts. In Burri's case, the material is inherent, sublimated, almost excavated. It acts as a passage to another material world (p. 79). In Fontana, the slashing of the canvas is a prelude to another dimension. The sense of space is contained within the work, giving rise to elements which can be grouped together or remain independent (p. 93). The most immediate elements of Fontana's visual language are volume, colour, light, shadow and the modelling of three-dimensional form. All of these are visible in the structure of the work. This is not *a posteriori* abstraction but a deliberate distancing through which 'existence, nature and matter are all in perfect harmony'.[51] Certainly the *tagli* and *buchi* demonstrate this unity of dynamic elements, where the *nature* sculptures seem to contain energy, as though a picture had closed in on itself for self-protection (p. 111).

It is possible then, as Crispolti has proposed, to think in terms of a 'Burri–Fontana axis' which, in the years in question, posed 'an alternative, problematic dialectic around the stumbling-block of existential naturalist ... *Informel*'.[52] This axis provided the foundations for the *Arte Povera* of Mario Merz, Michelangelo Pistoletto, Jannis Kounellis and Pino Pascali, by reducing the sign to basics and rewriting it, in order then to restore it to its archetypal status. Furthermore, this axis acted as a counterbalance to other contemporary experiences and mythologies, such as the readymade and drip-painting, and incorporated elements from Action Painting, *Art Autre* (as formulated by Michel Tapié) and *Informel*, in which the sign was read as being part of the transformation of the consistency of materials.

Burri's and Fontana's use of matter shook the foundations of the Italian art world. Kounellis shed light on the aftershock when he stated that 'the vision of the heap of coals is apocalyptic and forces us to re-examine the past in a new way'. Of the materiality of Fautrier, Pollock, Tàpies, Burri and Fontana, Kounellis added that their obsession with substance is a point of convergence for essentially fragile and dramatic outlooks, 'in order not to lose the thread of a discussion in favour of an acceptable and positive modernity against an uncritical and sentimental traditionalism.'[53]

> The artist must confront these myths and reduce them, by means of amorphous and confused materials, to clear images. Since these are atavistic forces that have their origins in the subconscious, the work of art takes on a magical significance. On the other hand, art has always had a religious value, from the first artist-sorcerer to the pagan and Christian myth, etc.
> (Piero Manzoni, *Per la scoperta di una zona d'immagini*, manuscript, 1957)

> There is nothing further to add: there is only to be, to live.
> (Piero Manzoni, *Azimuth*, 1960)

Piero Manzoni's first pictorial experiments date back to 1956. They reveal a Jungian-inspired metaphysical anxiety and a longing to achieve a materiality that goes beyond any preconceived form, reworked by artists; something that is complete in itself, that *is*. In his manifesto *Per la scoperta di una zona d'immagini* (For the discovery of a zone of images), dated 9 December 1956, he wrote:

> Without myth there is no art. The picture is our idea of freedom; in its space we set out on a journey of discovery and creation of images ... The work of art is born out of an unconscious impulse, the origin and death of a collective substratum, but the artistic event rests in our awareness of the gesture.[54]

Within a year, between December 1956 and November 1957, this first declaration was followed by six manifestos and two manuscripts in which Manzoni reworked his conception of art. It was a *terra incognita*, where matter, gesture, the mind, the picture itself existed in so far as it was an 'area of freedom in which we search for the discovery of our first images'.[55]

In Manzoni's artistic production, this was the moment of the *ominidi* or hominids, in which can still be seen the two primary elements of energy released from matter and vitality of gesture. He subordinated once again – but from a different perspective – the relation of the object to the subject, of the inorganic to the organic, the viewer to the creator. These little-known works represent a transitional phase. Little by little matter came to predominate, while the archaic representational image, the nightmare of a past that has its roots in the archetypes and the collective unconscious, faded into the shadows.

Manzoni felt the need to break this vicious circle, by now abused and corrupted. In his first 1958 *achromes* he made an effort to give shape to the inner energy of the picture, to see something for what it is. In other words he sought to bring art back to its original condition so that the picture could become a virgin space, a blank point of departure.

Such depersonalisation in conceiving and making art implies a concept of the truth which differs entirely from metaphysics. In ancient Greek, the word for truth was *aléteia*, where the initial 'alpha' places a negative value on the verb *lanthàno,* which means 'to be' or 'to remain obscure'. This is the meaning that Manzoni accepts.[56] The *achrome* is a pure physical entity, pure truth, a pure display of raw canvas soaked in and stiffened by kaolin. Art should no longer be mediated by the artist's interpretative code; art is pure visual language, immediate, without gesture or narrative. It is the 'alpha' of the new alphabet, which leads not to reasoning but to existence itself, to a zone of feeling beyond anything subjective or objective, active or passive. The difference cannot be appreciated solely by means of conceptual explanation or philological interpretation, even less through enraptured inspiration. Thus: 'Why not seek to discover the unlimited meaning of total space, of pure and absolute light?'[57]

Manzoni was well aware of the pitfalls of his chosen course of action and of the uneasiness which both spectators and critics would experience in trying to understand his work:

> Let's be clear, appreciating a painting or any work of art does not mean to understand the subject but to recognise its inner significance. A painting is a means of communication, not a luxurious addition to interior design; a painting has always been a magical object, a religious object. ... The artist is a forerunner: he reveals new totems and taboos of which his contemporaries may harbour the seed but of which they are not yet aware.[58]
>
> In order to understand these pre-conscious universal myths and make them his own, the artist (oh, what an abused and vilified word!) must reach his own individual mythology in that zone where it can become identified with universal mythology.[59]

His concept of mythology needs to be revised and put into context. Manzoni is not referring to classical mythology, but to a contemporary mythology where even industrial cast-offs can be mythologised just as well as any personal organic by-products.

Manzoni can be seen as the point of convergence for a material thematic, but at the same time as a point of departure for an international dialogue on the subject. His *achromes* definitively destroy that code which in painting made a distinction between structural and figurative elements. A painting is the pictorial representation of something; it depicts a subject constructed from things that are analogous to objects from everyday sensory

Piero Manzoni
Achrome, 1962
Panini (bread rolls) and kaolin, 39 × 39 cm
Catalogo generale: 1019 (see p. 135)
Private collection

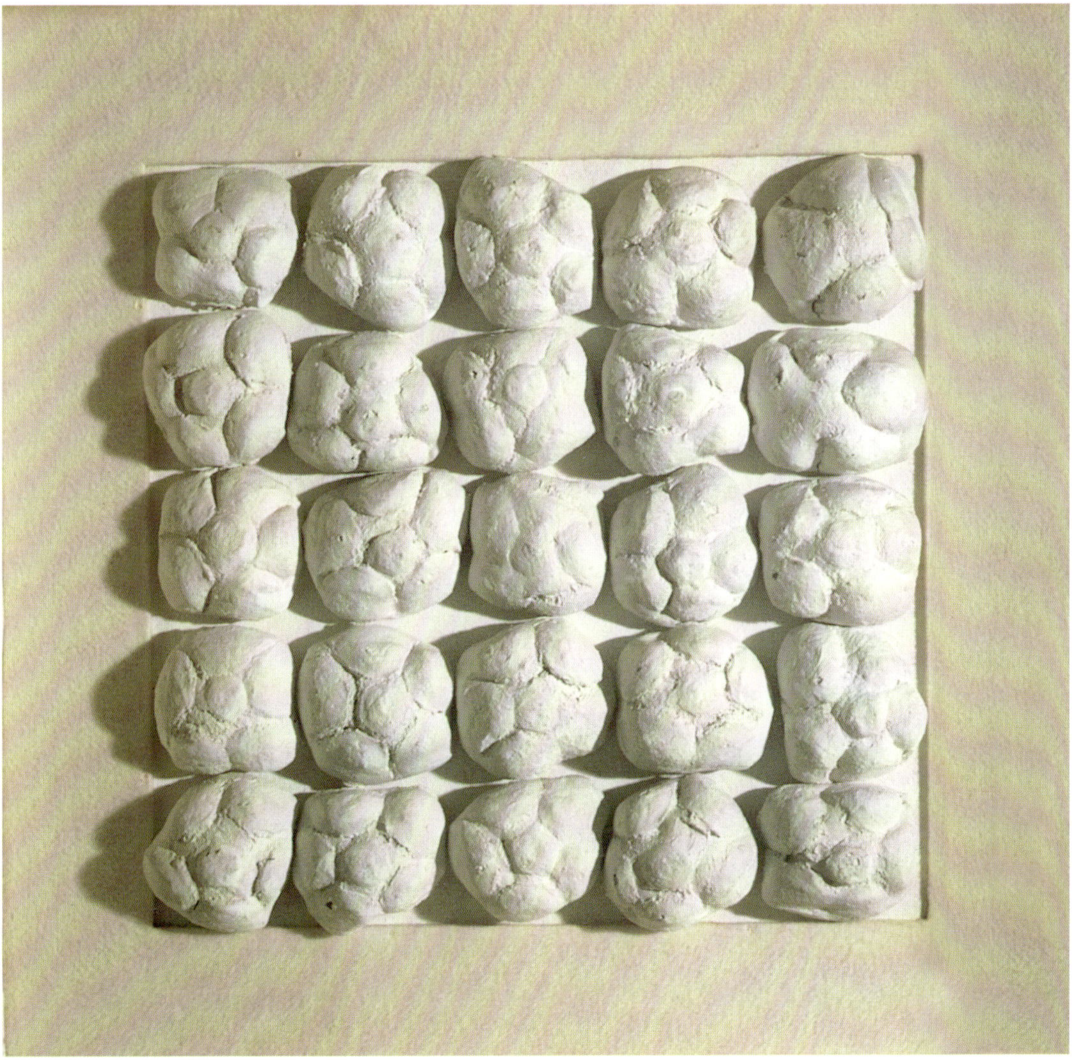

experience. Moreover a picture is organised according to rules and structural concepts that belong only to painting. Other artists had totally subverted these concepts and representations, but here we encounter a different paradigm. Manzoni turns the very surface of the painting into symbolic form: what was a structural element – he called it a *medium* – had become the primary image, the new totem. This marks the break with an association between a linguistic stimulus (in this case the painting) and its visual interpreter (the viewer), in what is a semiotic recognition of the image as derived from the viewer's culture at that precise historical moment.[60]

It seems inconceivable, from a logical point of view, to imagine entities that man does not convert into signs but which are and remain entities, zones of freedom. The *achromes* neutralise: 'two harmonising colours or two tones of the same colour are already sufficient to create a relationship extraneous to the significance of the surface which is unique, limitless and absolutely dynamic.'[61] The canvas was not painted over but soaked with matter, and was not finished by the artist but left to dry by itself. This was one of Manzoni's innovations. Up to now a mere tool of the artist, the canvas became significant in itself but with a different meaning (it may sound like a play on words), that is in fact devoid of meaning, as the existential flow has been stemmed. The *achromes* represent only the first step in this 'theory of discharges' which would become pivotal within the artist's quest. Manzoni, after singling out a *zone of encounter*, an *area of freedom*, would concern himself with discharges such as his own artist's breath, artist's blood, artist's fingerprints and artist's shit, where flow became identified with the secretions of his own body.

This typically Manzonian materiality found common ground with groups (such as *Zero* and *Phases*) and individuals (such as Enrico Castellani and Jan Schoonhoven) whose activities encompassed Germany, Belgium, Holland and Italy rather than France. The exception is Yves Klein, and it is necessary here to clarify the relationship between him and Manzoni, who is sometimes erroneously described as his follower. Manzoni's entire ideology contrasted with the Frenchman's. Klein was constantly drawn to a Being, immanent and cosmic, whose existence precedes any concrete manifestation. His is a mystical, ascetic viewpoint, inclined towards a cosmology that is transcendental and absolute. In his *Blue Revolution* he believed in 'a movement aiming to transform the way of thinking and acting of an audience'.[62] Elsewhere, he added: 'We will know the force of attraction towards the high realms, towards space, towards nowhere and everywhere both at once. The force of terrestrial attraction thus mastered we will literally levitate in total physical and spiritual freedom.'[63] While Klein's impulse was, therefore, ascensional and vertical, Manzoni's was horizontal, focused on what is all-pervading, base and corporeal, even while trying to deify it and imbue it with brief flashes of eternity and artistry. For Klein, art was a cathartic force the purpose of which was to free the world of all contact with objects; whereas 'materialism has been acknowledged as the enemy of freedom and psychology, sentimentality and composition are also very real enemies'.[64] His blue monochromes are not made as objective representations but in order to resolve abstraction, in order to conquer infinite space and lose oneself within it. His *International Klein Blue* is only a contingent and concrete trace leading to a cosmic state, 'the omnipotent blue'. Considered from a psychoanalytic perspective following Norman Brown, Klein championed sublimation and death while Manzoni vigorously supported the ego-flesh and therefore life itself.[65]

Manzoni's development surely also owes some debt to Jean Fautrier's *Otages* (hostages) and the nature of this debt is linguistic and structural rather than emotional. In contrast to Fautrier's anguish and turmoil, Manzoni's *achromes* are ascetic and emotionless, simply by being there and not aspiring to be anything else. Moreover, the Italian places himself in opposition to the spiritual search of certain European or Japanese groups, like *Nul* or *Gutaï*, while acknowledging their own particular brand of magic.

Manzoni and Castellani founded the periodical *Azimuth* (later also the name of their art gallery, *Azimut*) as a privileged arena for avant-garde exchanges and debates. It sought 'to state and make known the *modus operandi* adopted by art movements whose cultural development revealed a strong irrational trend (*Informel*), with gestural connotations influenced by American art and associated with the residual influence of Dada and Surrealism'.[66] A number of other publications had set the tone including *Il gesto* (initiated by Enrico Baj and Sergio Dangelo) and *Mac espace*, the manifestos of *Spazialismo* and *Arte Nucleare*, and, abroad, *Zero* in Düsseldorf (founded by Heinz Mack, Otto Piene and Günther Uecker) and *Nul* in Amsterdam. 'The way of divulging the ideological aims of various groups is clearly derived from the publicising precedents set by the historic avant-garde, above all Futurism.'[67] Once again it was considered necessary to refer to the historic avant-garde movements 'in order to escape the cultural ghetto of Fascism which had given life to an artificial post-Cubism with socialist undertones, and to a debased Surrealism worthy only of being exhibited in a butcher's shop'.[68]

Castellani and Manzoni were following almost identical paths in this period. Their artistic development had a keen observer in Fontana who, according to Castellani 'was the person most interested in young people. Manzoni said that it was more the youngsters who gave to Fontana than the other way round!'[69] Castellani was already working with a hemming machine while Manzoni was fixing handkerchief-like squares to canvas with plaster. He showed a keen interest in Manzoni's monochromes and in his experiments with light effects on the ridges and indentations of the single-coloured material surfaces. Manzoni's artistic quest always led him to push onwards, to extend his production, without compromising either his desire to experiment or his move towards an essential reductiveness (as seen in his early *ominidi*).

His first paintings of 1957 were canvases soaked in kaolin, but in September 1958 Manzoni's *achromes* prepared for his solo show in Rotterdam underwent a major change.[70] Square pieces of canvas soaked in kaolin and glue were arranged on canvases that were generally rectangular (p. 105). The association of rectangular and square forms became the starting point for an investigation into the proportional relationship of the white surface. In 1959, the structural 'raster', as he called it,[71] of the *achromes* consisted of machine-stitched seams. Others were made of polystyrene or impregnated with cobalt chloride, which change colour under different climatic conditions.

Before considering the later part of Manzoni's work, this fundamental phase in his creative process must be grasped, as he moved slowly from the material object, a place of being, to a use of matter that was personal and organic. Having argued that a 'painting has a value only inasmuch as it is a totality',[72] Manzoni needed a space in which to project his own self, to fulfil his role as a sorcerer, to identify art with his corporeal fragments and with the notion of matter-time-space.

In 1959 he set to work on the *linee* (lines). These translated the concept of space-time into a visible object. The link between matter and time was forged at the very moment of creating the work of art, which was then parcelled in a sealed container, labelled with the length of the line, the area covered and the time taken to produce it. Time thus is evident as the work of art. The *linee* exemplified the idea of the void – one was immediately purchased by Fontana – and the absolute elimination of anything superfluous. They are reduced to what they are, the fundamental principle of making art. Finite lines led to *Linee infinite*, based on the same idea but then represented only by the box: a tube made of wood and painted black with a label to indicate the contents.

The well-known *Tavole d'accertamento* (verification pictures) were completed in 1959. These are simply reproductions of familiar modes of communication, such as the alphabet and maps. At the same time Manzoni made another leap forward when he created the *Corpi d'aria* (Bodies of air): inflated sculptures eighty centimetres in diameter and, with the base, 120 centimetres in height. These could be purchased filled with the *fiato d'artista* (artist's breath); when inflated by Manzoni each became a unique piece of art. This 'verification' results in the body and corporeal products and traces becoming the material of art. Manzoni was, therefore, not selling an idea,[73] a journey into another dimension, or a ticket to eternity, but a by-product of his own body. He planned to sell phials of his own blood and tins of his own shit, sharing his 'personal sacrifice' with the public. From this starting point would develop the repetitive and commercialised mass-production of the work of art.[74] As one commentator observed: 'In contrast to Duchamp, Manzoni would never, even in his wildest dreams, have called his productions works of art. He denied the concept of art, and put himself forward as the ultimate focus of our attention.'[75]

Another series of imprints are those Manzoni made on eggs which were then transformed into *Sculture da mangiare* (Edible sculptures), making an even more direct relationship between the work of art and the viewer.[76] These were the subject of the last Happening at the Galleria Azimut: *Consumazione dell'arte dinamica del pubblico divorare l'arte* (Consumption of dynamic art by the art-devouring public). Germano Celant has commented: 'The language of the body is drawn into the search for understanding and becomes historical evidence.'[77]

On 13 January 1961 Manzoni began signing not only his own body but other peoples' bodies. Marking a move from the subjective to the objective, these were true *living sculptures*, bodies made works of art purely because they were signed by the artist. The accompanying certificate of authenticity turned the impermanent signature into a permanent artwork. Manzoni made use of a variety of related strategies, including acquisition, to denote something as a work of art. One of these was his *base magica* (magic base), a simple pedestal which temporarily transforms whoever stands on it into a work of art; on stepping off, he or she returns to the anonymous mass.

Let us turn, finally, to a different aspect of matter, to the *achromes* produced after this experimentation with the corporeal. In 1961 Manzoni made a series of works, which became known as *nuvole* (clouds), made from glass fibre (p. 115). Happy to use both synthetic and natural materials, he also made a series of works using balls of cotton wool aligned geometrically, which are very close in appearance to his early white paintings (p. 87). In other works he used polystyrene (p. 121), which at times acquired almost transcendental qualities (certainly in spite of the artist's intentions). Both polystyrene and the small plastic discs he used in other works were chosen for their immersion in the immanence of concrete fact. Distinctive also – though certainly not to be aligned in any way with Pop art – are his *panini* (bread rolls), small, flower-shaped rolls encrusted and stuck onto canvas (p. 43). Known as *michette* or *rosette* (rosettes), these are the daily bread eaten by all and, therefore, part of the language of everyday life in Italy. Manzoni's *panini* result in an unexpected stasis, an automatism consecrated to art, imbued with an anxiety of repetition.

It is not possible to know what more might have happened in the adventure into and about matter had Manzoni not died prematurely, aged twenty-nine. In Amsterdam for an exhibition of the *Zero* group, he conceived and embarked upon a new sculpture in collaboration with Henk Peeters entitled *Il mare* (The sea), which would have consisted of seawater contained in a cylinder. Having journeyed from the synthetic to the corporeal perhaps he would have ended with the natural; who can say? Certainly, natural materials and/or functional objects are the new matter (from *Arte Povera* onwards) out of which were built the dreams of what we still call art, which itself is 'like a cavern behind which there is another deeper cave, a world more vast, more strange, richer below the surface, an abyss below every piece of firm ground, beyond every known foundation.'[78]

Translated by Michela Parkin

[1] Umberto Boccioni, *Première exposition de sculpture futuriste du peintre et sculpteur futuriste Boccioni*, exh. cat., Galerie Le Boëtie, Paris 1913, republished in *Pittura-scultura futurista* (*Dinamismo plastico*), Edizioni Futuriste di 'Poesia', Milan 1914, p. 211; trans. modified from Ida Gianelli, 'Chronology', in Pontus Hulten and Germano Celant (eds.), *Italian Art 1900–1945*, Bompiani, Milan 1989, p. 615.

[2] Umberto Boccioni, letter quoted by Piero Buscaroli in *La vista, l'udito e la memoria,* Fogola, Turin 1987, p. 142. See also Maurizio Calvesi, Rosella Siligato and Marzio Pinottini, *Dal futurismo al laser,* exh. cat., Palau de la Virreina, Barcelona, Mazzotta, Milan 2000.

[3] Filippo Tommaso Marinetti, *Manifesto tecnico della letteratura futurista,* Direzione del Movimento Futurista, Edizioni Futuriste, Milan 1914, trans. modified from R.W. Flint (ed.), *Marinetti: Selected Writings*, Secker and Warburg, London 1972, p. 87.

[4] Giacomo Balla and Fortunato Depero, *Ricostruzione futurista dell'universo,* Direzione del Movimento Futurista, Edizioni Futuriste, Milan, 11 March 1915.

[5] Filippo Tommaso Marinetti, *Lo splendore geometrico meccanico e la sensibilità numerica: Manifesto futurista,* Direzione del Movimento Futurista, Edizioni Futuriste, Milan, 18 March 1914.

[6] Christine Poggi, *In Defiance of Painting,* Yale University Press, New Haven and London 1992.

[7] 'Libera dimensione / Free

Dimension / Libre dimension' (text in Italian, English and French), *Azimuth*, no. 2, 1960, p. 19.
[8] *Il Tattilismo, Manifesto futurista,* Direzione del Movimento Futurista, Milan 1921. Attention is focused on the importance of 'educating the touch to the point of intensity through an educative scale of touch which is, at the same time, a scale of tactile values for Tactilism or the Art of Touch. ... First category: abstract touch ... silver paper, glass paper; second category: persuasive touch ... smooth silk.'
[9] Carlo Carrà, *Pittura metafisica,* Vallecchi, Florence 1919, trans. modified from Massimo Carrà (ed.), *Metaphysical Art*, Thames and Hudson, London 1971, p. 48.
[10] Enrico Prampolini, 'Arte polimaterica (Verso un'arte collettiva?)', in *Anticipazioni,* Edizioni del Secolo, Rome 1944.
[11] Ibid.
[12] Ibid.
[13] Ibid.
[14] Ibid.
[15] Germano Celant, 'Dal millenovecentocinquanta al millenovecentosettanta', in *Catalogo generale dell'opera di Piero Manzoni*, Skira, Milan 2004, p. LXX.
[16] Milton Gendel, in conversation with Anna Costantini, Rome, 13 February 1993, in Germano Celant, *Rome–New York 1948–1964: An Art Exploration*, exh. cat., Murray and Isabella Rayburn Foundation, New York 1993, p. 54.
[17] From the manifesto signed by Capogrossi, Ballocco, Colla, Burri, cited in ibid., p. 62.
[18] Unsigned editorial, *Arti Visive: Rivista della Fondazione Origine*, July–Aug. 1952, front [p. 1].
[19] Alberto Moravia, *Twenty Imaginary Views of the American Scene by Twenty Young Italian Artists*, exh. cat., De Luca, Rome 1953.
[20] Quoted in Hereward L. Cooke, *Accardi,* exh. cat., Galleria San Marco, Rome, June 1955.
[21] Piero Dorazio, 'New Italian Art: A Promise', *Art Digest*, no. 28, July 1954, pp. 10–1.
[22] Ibid.
[23] Dore Ashton, 'The Artist in Europe', *New York Times Magazine*, 8 May 1955.
[24] Remo Bianco, *Manifesto dell'Arte Improntale*, Milan 1956.
[25] Emilio Villa, 'Alberto Burri', *Arti Visive*, nos. 4–5, May 1953, pp. 4–5; trans. in Celant 1993, pp. 80–1.
[26] Alberto Burri, *Parola di Burri,* ed. Stefano Zorzi, Allemandi, Turin 1995; see also Marco Vallora, *I "neri" di Burri,* Mazzotta, Milan 2003.
[27] Ibid., p. 176.
[28] Ibid., p. 83.
[29] Emilio Villa, *Attributi dell'arte odierna 1947–1967,* Feltrinelli, Milan 1970; see also Maurizio Calvesi and Rosella Siligato, *Roma anni '60: Al di là della pittura*, Edizioni Carte Segrete, Rome 1990.
[30] James Johnson Sweeney, *Burri,* exh. cat., L'Obelisco, Rome 1955, and *Alberto Burri,* exh. cat., Carnegie Institute, Pittsburgh 1957.
[31] André Pieyre de Mandiargues, 'Burri', *La Nouvelle Revue Française*, Aug. 1954.
[32] See, for instance: James P. Byrnes, *The Collages of Alberto Burri,* exh. cat., Fine Arts Center, Colorado Springs 1955; Michel Tapié, *Burri et César*, exh. cat., Galerie Rive Droite, Paris 1956; Paul Wember, *Alberto Burri,* Museum Haus Lange, Krefeld 1959; Herbert Read, *Alberto Burri,* exh. cat., Hanover Gallery, London 1960.
[33] See Francesco Arcangeli, *Alberto Burri. Dal Romanticismo all'informale,* Einaudi, Turin 1977; Giulio Carlo Argan, *Burri,* exh. cat., Palais des Beaux-Arts, Brussels 1959.
[34] Maurizio Calvesi, *Le due avanguardie,* Laterza, Rome-Bari 1975.
[35] Enrico Crispolti, *Alberto Burri. Mostra antologica: Opere dal 1948 al 1955*, exh. cat., Galleria La Medusa, Rome 1961.
[36] Cesare Brandi, *Burri,* exh. cat., Galleria Marlborough, Rome 1962.
[37] Lucio Fontana, 'Ultima intervista in vita (Comabbio 19 luglio 1968)', ed. Tommaso Trini, in Bruno Corà (ed.), *Burri e Fontana 1949–1968*, exh. cat., Skira, Milan 1996.
[38] Ibid.; see also 'The Last Interview Given by Fontana', *Studio*

International, Nov. 1972, pp. 15–6.
[39] Umberto Boccioni, *Pittura-scultura futurista (Dinamismo plastico)*, Edizioni Futuriste di 'Poesia', Milan 1914, chapter on *Complementarismo dinamico.*
[40] Statement in the special re-edition of the *Manifiesto blanco*, Galleria Apollinaire, Milan 1968.
[41] The *Manifiesto blanco* was signed by Bernardo Arias, Horacio Cazenueve, Marcos Fridman, Pablo Arias, Rodolfo Burgos, Enrique Benito, Cesar Bernal, Luis Coll, Alfredo Hansen and Jorge Rocamonte. Fontana did not sign because of his position as a sculpture tutor in Buenos Aires at the Escuela Nacional de Bellas Artes, Manuel Belgrano, as well as at the Altamira Escuela Libre de Artes Plasticas. The latter, funded by Gonzalo Losada, was formed by groups of exiled Spanish intellectuals. Emilio Pettoruti, friend of Carlo Carrà and Gino Severini, taught painting there and the school was closely associated with the avant-garde movement *Madí*, which grew out of the Movimento d'Arte Concretista.
[42] Lucio Fontana, Giorgio Kaisserlian, Beniamino Joppolo and Milena Milani, *Primo manifesto dello spazialismo,* Milan 1947.
[43] Ibid.
[44] Lucio Fontana, 'Ultima intervista', in Corà 1996.
[45] Ibid.
[46] Ibid.
[47] Lucio Fontana, 'Dichiarazione', in *Lucio Fontana*, exh. cat., Galleria del Naviglio, Milan 1953, cited in Enrico Crispolti, *Centenario di Lucio Fontana,* Charta, Milan 1999. See also George Kubler, *The Shape of Time,* Yale University Press, New Haven and London 1972.
[48] Quoted in Jole de Sanna, *Lucio Fontana: materia, spazio, concetto*, Mursia, Milan 1993. On the same theme Fontana stated: 'Art is always Art, whatever expression it takes, but that expression can revolutionise Art'; draft of a letter to Giampiero Gianni, Albisola, 2 Nov. 1949, cited in Paolo Campiglio (ed.), *Lucio Fontana: Lettere 1919–1968*, Skira, Milan 1999, p. 243.
[49] Umberto Boccioni, *Pittura-scultura futurista (Dinamismo plastico)*, Edizioni Futuriste di 'Poesia', Milan 1914.
[50] Umberto Eco considered this question in 'Il problema dell'opera aperta' (The difficulty of open art) presented at the XII Congresso Internazionale di Filosofia (12th International conference of philosophy) 1958; see also Enrico Crispolti, *Lucio Fontana: Catalogo generale,* Electa, Milan 1986.
[51] *Primo manifesto dello spazialismo,* Milan 1947.
[52] Enrico Crispolti, 'Un Asse Burri-Fontana?', in Corà 1996, pp. 49–50; trans. modified from p. 56.
[53] Bruno Corà, 'Conversazione con Jannis Kounellis su Burri e Fontana', in ibid. p. 85; trans. modified from p. 87.
[54] Piero Manzoni, Camillo Corvi-Mova, Ettore Sordini and Giuseppe Zecca, *Per la scoperta di una zona d'immagini,* Milan, 9 Dec. 1956. A manuscript of the same title survives from 1957; see next note.
[55] Second, manuscript, version of *Per la scoperta di una zona d'immagini*, [spring] 1957; trans. in Germano Celant, *Piero Manzoni*, exh. cat., Serpentine Gallery, London 1998, p. 54.
[56] See Mario Perniola, *L'estetica del Novecento,* Il Mulino, Bologna 1997.
[57] Piero Manzoni, 'Libera dimensione', *Azimuth*, no. 2, Milan 1960, trans. in Celant 1998, p. 130.
[58] Piero Manzoni, *Ricerca d'immagine,* 1957, republished in Germano Celant, *Piero Manzoni: Catalogo generale*, Skira, Milan 2004, p. 33.
[59] Piero Manzoni, 'Prolegomeni per un'attività artistica', March 1957, published on the occasion of his solo exhibition at the Galleria del Corriere della Provincia, Como, December 1957.
[60] See Umberto Eco, *La struttura assente,* Electa, Milan 1968.
[61] Piero Manzoni, 'Libera dimensione', *Azimuth*, no. 2, Milan 1960, trans. in Celant 1998, p. 131.
[62] Yves Klein, 'Esquisse et grandes lignes du système économique de la révolution bleue', Berlin 1961, trans. in Sidra Stich, *Yves Klein*, exh. cat., Hayward Gallery, London 1995, pp. 145–6.
[63] Yves Klein, lecture to coincide with the exhibition of Jean Tinguely in

Düsseldorf in January 1959; trans. ibid., p. 159. For more detail see Celant 2004.
[64] Yves Klein and Werner Ruhnau, 'Création d'un centre de la sensibilité', Gelsenkirchen, 27 March 1959, quoted in Stich 1995, p. 123.
[65] Norman Brown, *Life Against Death,* Wesleyan University Press, Middletown 1959.
[66] The press release, cited in Celant 2004 p. 650, reads: 'The articles in the first publication *Azimuth* are by V. Agnetti, B. Alfieri, G. Ballo, G. Dorfles, A. Galvano, F. Picabia, K. Schwitters and Y. Tono. As well as reproductions of works by thirty-two Italian and foreign painters and sculptors ... inserted in the text: *Peinture executée en collaboration avec metà-matic n° 12 de Tinguely*, a drawing made by Jean Tinguely using an automatic drawing machine which produced a drawing when a token was inserted.'
[67] Yet another reference to Futurism rather than later readings and elaborations of it. On this same theme *Miriorama 1*, an exhibition organised by the Gruppo *T*, opened on 15 January 1960 in Milan. In its first session readings took place of texts by Boccioni, Balla, Depero, Klee and Fontana.
[68] Bruno Corà, 'Conversazione con Enrico Castellani', in Corà 1996, p. 72, trans. modified from p. 74.
[69] Ibid.
[70] In Rotterdam, the artist Gust Romijin introduced him to Hans Sonneberger.
[71] 'Raster' is a German word, used in the field of typography to indicate the typographer's screen or to describe the lines and bars of colour on a television screen.
[72] Piero Manzoni, 'Libera dimensione', *Azimuth*, no. 2, Milan 1960, trans. in Celant 1998, p. 131.
[73] Though see the quotation cited under 'Greenwich Meridian' in Matthew Gale's 'From Alphabet to Zone', below (p. 97).
[74] Piero Manzoni in a letter to Addi Køpke, his dealer in Copenhagen, suggested that in order to render his *corpi d'aria* more saleable, the gallery should keep them away from direct sunlight and dust them with talcum powder (Sohn of Marck Archive, Groningen).
[75] Otto Schwalbe, *Cubisme til informel kunst,* Borgen 1961.
[76] Piero Manzoni, letter to Giampaolo Macentelli, 1962, Manzoni Archive, Milan: 'In certain productions dating from 1960 I raised hard-boiled eggs to the status of art: the public was able to have a direct contact with these works by swallowing whole works of art over a period of 70 minutes'.
[77] Celant 2004.
[78] Friedrich Nietzsche, *Thus Spoke Zarathustra,* Penguin, Harmondsworth 1961.

pp. 53–4 (recto and verso)
Alberto Burri
Combustione, 1963, *Combustion*
Plastic and combustion on aluminium stretcher, 55 × 46 cm
Catalogo sistematico: 701 (see p. 135)
Fondazione Palazzo Albizzini 'Collezione Burri', Città di Castello

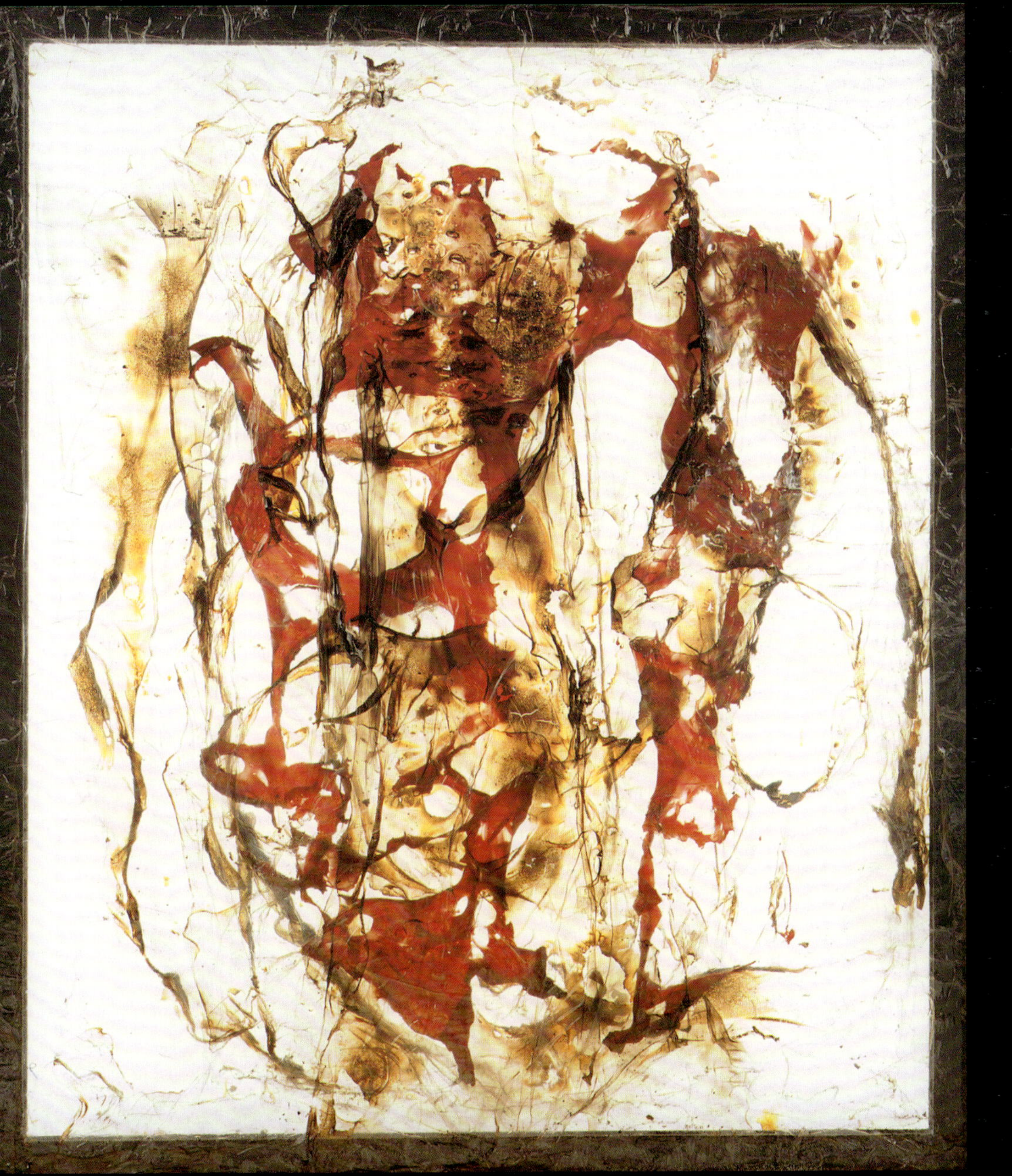

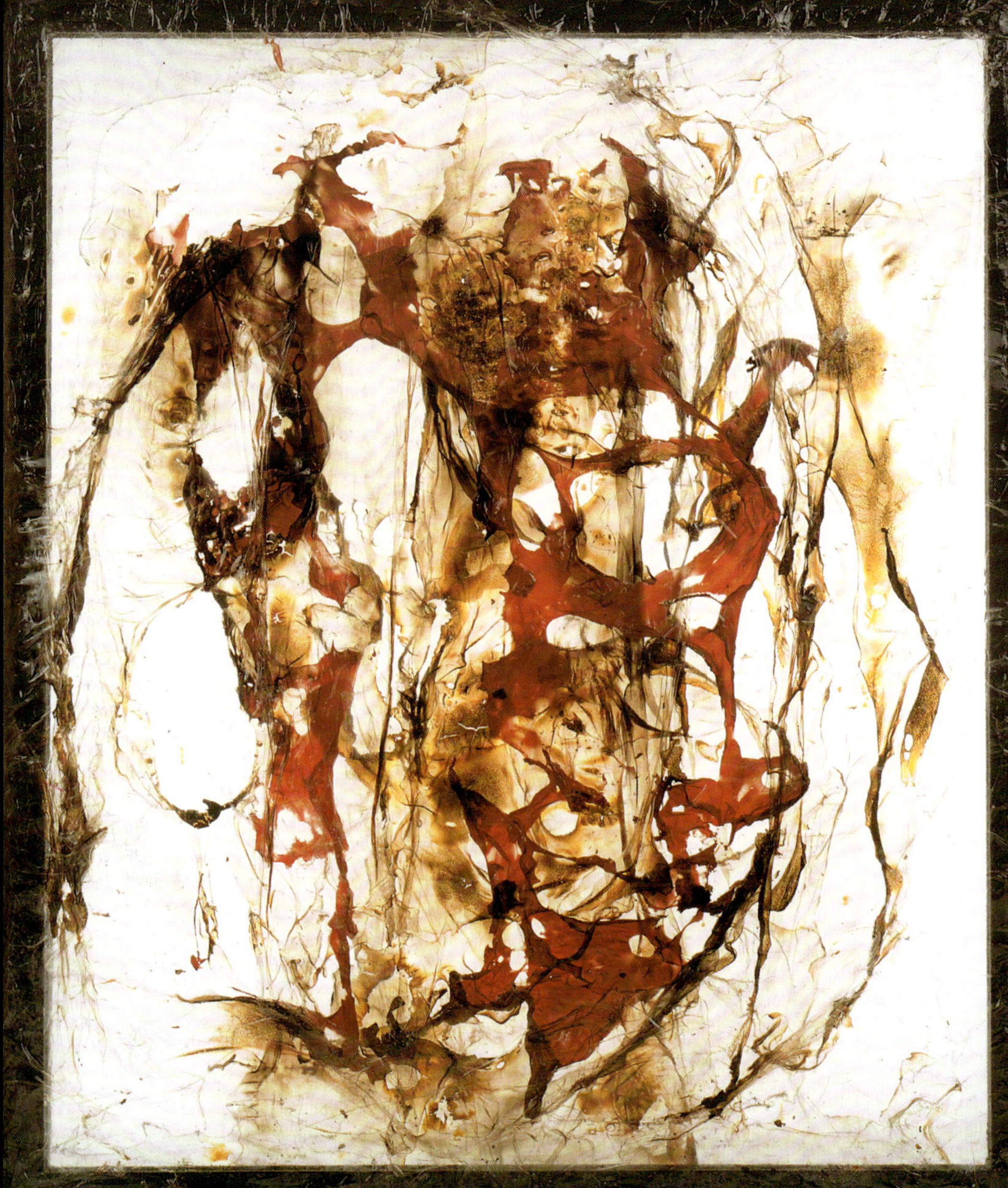

From Alphabet to Zone

Matthew Gale

In late 1956 Piero Manzoni was a co-signatory to a manifesto entitled *Per la scoperta di una zona d'immagini* (For the discovery of a zone of images).[1] Opening with the declaration that 'without myth there is no art',[2] the text was charged with ideas derived from Jungian psychoanalysis. It proposed the power of a shared mythology as a rich seam for individual artistic production. It rejected the physical energies of the Abstract Expressionism of Jackson Pollock or Georges Mathieu's *Informel*. However, the authors believed that the work of art should be autonomous, and had no need to be linked to, or derive from, the visible world. In so doing, they declared: 'Our mode is an alphabet of prime images.'[3]

Between this 'alphabet' and the 'zone' of the manifesto's title lies surprising latitude. The former implies taxonomic order, while the latter allows for a more amorphous exploration within circumscribed boundaries. The texts that follow take their lead from this latitude, and adopt both strategies in addressing the work of Alberto Burri, Lucio Fontana and Piero Manzoni. The alphabetical ordering provides a structure for approaching a range of subjects relating to the artists and the period 1950–63. It also provides an outline within which to explore ideas in greater or lesser detail. There is no aspiration to be exhaustive (this is not a dictionary), but rather to bring together different levels of information that seem to have a practical, theoretical or circumstantial bearing. The propensity of each artist to work in series has been accommodated (with the original Italian names given precedence – hence *buchi* rather than *holes*) and linked specifically to those series represented in the exhibition's selection. The very abstraction of the structure – from alphabet to zone – allows for a flexibility that reflects the different theoretical positions adopted by these three innovators at the time.

In 1959, the critic and art historian Guido Ballo published an essay on Fontana entitled 'Beyond painting', from which we have taken our title. Ballo wrote: 'Freedom has become hope, optimism: the brilliance of a new mode of operating in harmony with the newest means of our times.'[4] This emphasis on optimism as part of innovation has been associated with Fontana, in particular, whose exploration of space may be compared to the paradoxical containment of infinity posited by the French philosopher Gaston Bachelard in his contemporary book *The Poetics of Space*. Bachelard provided a striking vision:

> Immensity is within ourselves. It is attached to a sort of expansion of being that life curbs and caution arrests, but which starts again when we are alone. As soon as we become motionless, we are elsewhere; we are dreaming in a world that is immense. Indeed, immensity is the movement of motionless man.[5]

This containment of space and motion may be seen as paralleling the experience of Fontana's passage into space, but perhaps – because the dimension is necessarily illusory – it is possible to see it as the reflection of the contemplative stasis experienced by the artist.

For many of their contemporaries such an 'intimate immensity' appeared as a debilitating void. An existential impossibility of communication, which haunted intellectuals even before the Second World War, seemed to be confirmed by the conflict and its atrocities. This is recognisably the obstacle that opens Alberto Moravia's novel *La noia* of 1961 (translated into English as *The Empty Canvas*).[6] The book begins with an artist recalling the laceration of a painting on which he had worked for many months. While this may read as a parody of Fontana's work, Moravia is concerned with the emptiness that precedes (and occasionally prevents) action. In front of a new blank canvas, the narrator realises that it 'was a particular canvas that I had placed on the easel at the termination of a long job of work.'

The extended decade of the 1950s – brought to a close with Manzoni's death in 1963 – was one of immense fertility in Italian art. The artists drawn together here were at the forefront of a formal and conceptual revolution that had international resonances and laid the groundwork for generations to come. Although independent (furthest apart in age, Fontana and Manzoni were closer by dint of geography), their paths crossed regularly so that Fontana was able to write of the other two in 1960: 'Manzoni … is a very intelligent boy who has already undertaken very important research in his art; of Burri, I am a friend and admirer.'[7] In looking back now, it is possible to recognise the energy with which they maintained a balance between existential anxiety and utopian optimism, as well as between political action and ironic distance.

Achrome

From 1957 Piero Manzoni produced *achromes*, works from which colour was eliminated in favour of white. This parallels a widely held desire to eradicate a narrative content in art that, even in the most abstract works, remained (in Manzoni's view at least) present through colour. In a key text of 1960, he explained:

> All problems of colour and all questions of chromatic relationships are also useless, even if one is only dealing with tonal modulations. We can only utilize a single colour or, rather, utilize a single uninterrupted and continuous surface from which anything superfluous and all interpretative possibilities are excluded. It is not a question of 'painting' blue on blue or white on white either in the sense of composing or of expressing oneself. In fact, quite the contrary. The question for me is that of creating an integrally white surface (yes, integrally colourless, neutral) which is completely unrelated to any pictorial phenomenon or to any element that is extraneous to the value of the surface. It is a white that is not a polar landscape, or a beautiful or evocative material, or a sensation, or a symbol, or anything else; it is a white surface that is nothing else but a white surface (a colourless surface that is nothing else but a colourless surface). Or, better still, it exists, and that is sufficient. It is, and to be totally is pure becoming.[8]

Manzoni set about his objective through a variety of strategies, each of which has evocative associations. It is probable that this paradox was not lost on him, as the very reductive nature of his work adopts, modifies and subverts practices already undertaken by contemporaries such as Burri, Fontana and Yves Klein.

As a demonstration of the reductive means of the artist, Manzoni began by soaking his canvases in kaolin – a soft china clay used in making porcelain and which he had discovered in the ceramic workshops in Albisola. The material's weight allowed him to abdicate judgements, to some extent (Celant claims that the canvas was 'transformed and completed by itself'),[9] over the form of folds and layers in the resulting image. The kaolin eliminated colour to the point of Manzoni's desired 'nothingness' but also unified the surface, which gained in density. The surfaces of the *achromes* made with kaolin have associations with the density of plaster used both in construction (for walls) and in medicine (for casting broken limbs).

As he recalled in his chronological account,[10] by 1959 Manzoni began to make *achromes* in other ways, including simply joining together pieces of white canvas. The structure offered by the stitch-lines provides a grid with residual echoes of Piet Mondrian's abstraction, but they reflect Manzoni's declaration of the

Piero Manzoni
Achrome, 1958–9
Kaolin on canvas, 110 × 150 cm
Catalogo generale: 348 (see p. 135)
Private collection

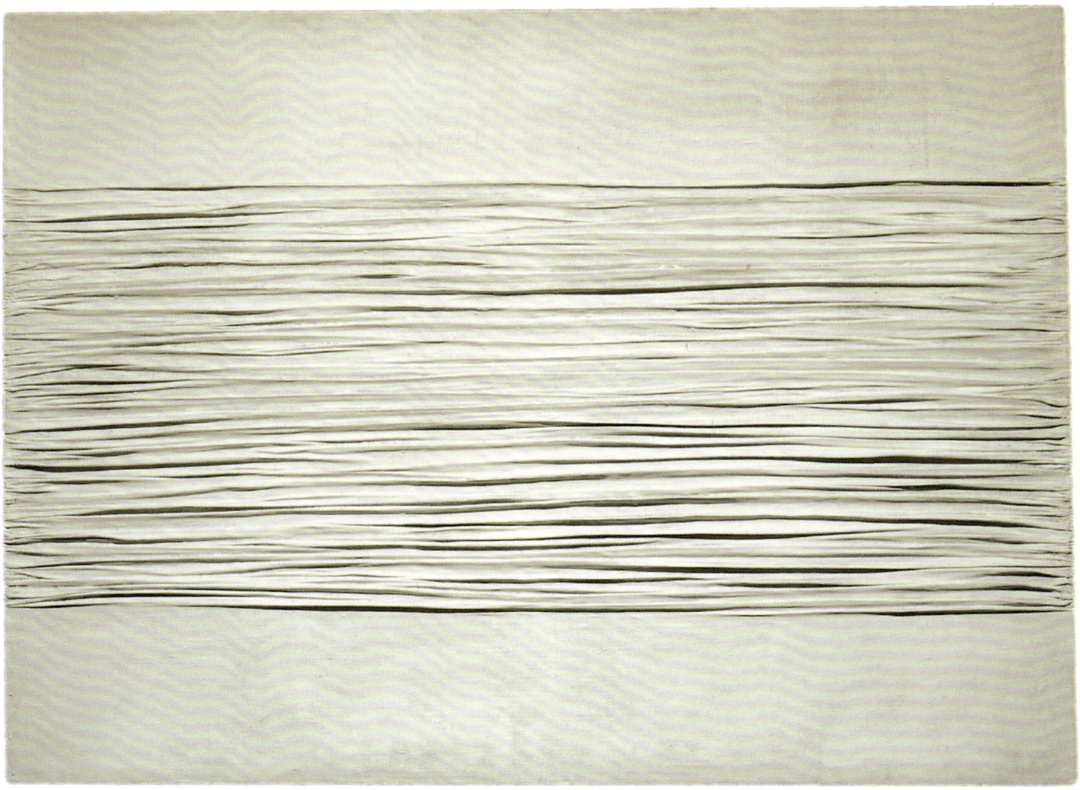

Lucio Fontana
Concetto spaziale, 1957, *Spatial Concept*
Oil and mixed media on canvas, 96 × 98 cm
Catalogo generale: 57 BA 1 (see p. 135)
Angelo and Silvia Calmarini collection

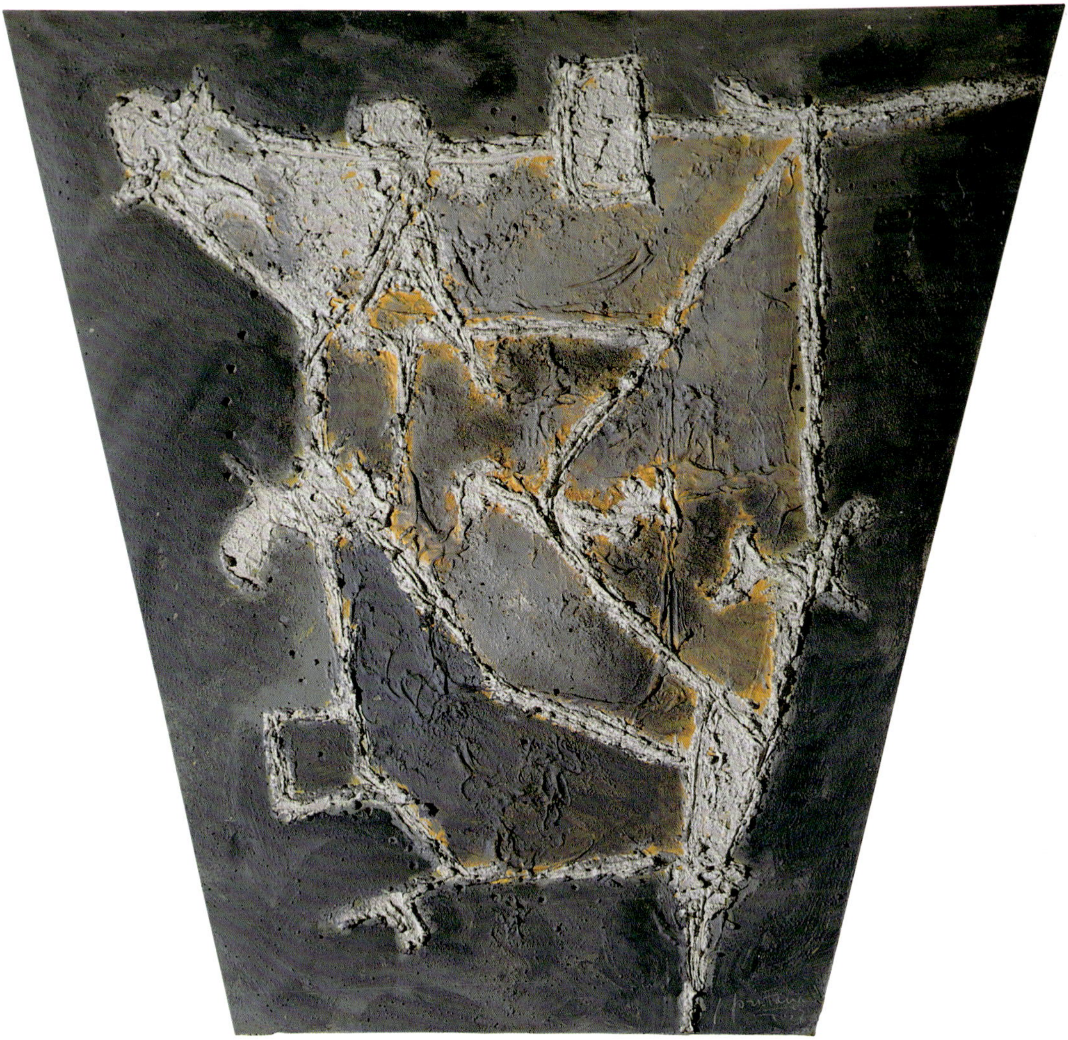

Alberto Burri
Bianco, 1952, *White*
Pumice stone, cloth and oil on canvas, 81 × 65 cm
Catalogo sistematico: 133 (see p. 135)
Fondazione Palazzo Albizzini 'Collezione Burri', Città di Castello

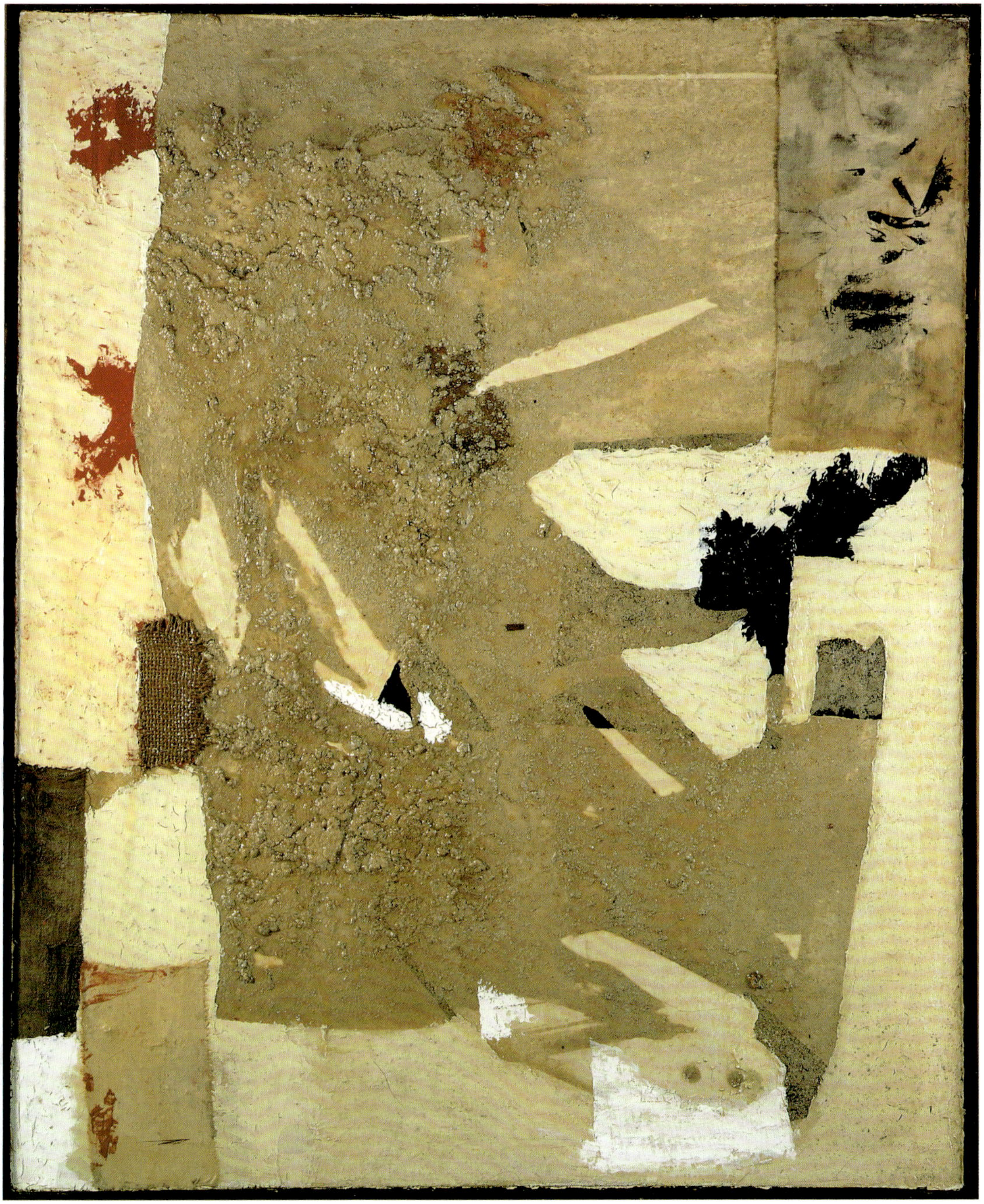

Alberto Burri
Nero, 1956, *Black*
Cloth, wire net and acrylic on canvas, 55 × 45 cm
Catalogo sistematico: 373 (see p. 135)
Fondazione Palazzo Albizzini 'Collezione Burri', Città di Castello

American colonialism. However, his interest was not simply a triumph of style over substance. As he makes clear, he understood that the Baroque had reflected a dynamic view of the universe underwritten by scientific discoveries. He argued that any new art should depart from a similar combination of existential awareness, scientific complexity and fertile creativity. The foundations of his *Spazialismo* were laid in Buenos Aires, where this response to Baroque combined with the constructivism of the *Madi* and associated groups and the avant-garde Academy of Altamira that Fontana helped to found. Movement was their conceptual point of departure; the passage quoted above continued: 'It is established that movement is an essential condition of matter as a beginning of the conception of the universe.' The *Manifiesto blanco* (White manifesto) of the previous year, published in Buenos Aires by Fontana's students and drafted with his help, posited just such a conjunction of analysis and creativity:

> Today experimental knowledge replaces imagined knowledge.
> We are aware of a world that exists and which is explained by itself and cannot be modified by our ideas.
> We are in need of an art whose value is contained within itself; an art uninfluenced by any idea we may have regarding it.[20]

The resultant autonomous art could also find precedents in the Baroque. A decade later, Fontana acknowledged this when in 1957 he augmented his *buchi* (holes; see p. 71) with the new series of *barocchi* (baroques; see p. 61). Their heavily laden surfaces seem to acknowledge and to parody both the exuberance of the Baroque and contemporary gestural abstraction. The puncturing of the canvas provides a counterpoint, extending the spatial dialogue between surface and depth. This highly individual approach was discussed by contemporary critics in terms of a 'neo-Baroque' conception of space but also had resonances with the gestural works of other artists associated with *Spazialismo* (notably Gianni Dova and Roberto Crippa).[21]

Black and white

The antimony between black and white has a long history in relation to the production of abstract art in the last one hundred years. Together they promise neutrality, even severity. The opposition of Kasimir Malevich's *White on White* by Alexandr Rodchenko's *Black on Black* in 1918, set the precedent.[22] By the 1940s and 1950s, black and white was seen in terms of restraint, even self-abnegation, in the work of artists such as Giuseppe Capogrossi, Willem De Kooning, Franz Kline and Pierre Soulages. The German artist Otto Piene wrote in *Azimuth* in 1960:

> Blackness in works of art is of two kinds: on the one hand it can be a sign, a symbol as in writing; on the other it can be the expression of desire for a colour-space. In the first case the black is the medium which makes the symbol visible and as such is justified, so long as the symbol itself has validity. In the second case, which one meets with repeatedly in recent years, the black is intended to express menace and mystery, the daemonic secret which is only guessed at. Black – like all dark colours tends to become the expression of the invisible as such.[23]

In the western tradition, white has a long association with purity, so that any intervention necessarily implies sullying. Burri's *bianchi* (whites) present a struggle between whiteness and colour, purity and impurity (p. 65). The surface bears a history, with the white acting to cover underlying layers and, in its failure to do so, proving revealing of that process. A more extreme manifestation of this tendency towards concealment is found in Manzoni's search for neutrality in the *achromes*.

Just as each also used white, Burri, Fontana and Manzoni all made works that were almost exclusively black. Burri's series of *neri* (blacks) antedate his *bianchi* and carry differing associations (p. 67). Their production resulted from encrustations of tar (the *catrami*) or black oil paint in which texture and surface are explored for their own qualities. Burri was certainly inspired by the parallel, though rather different, use of tar by Jean Dubuffet, whose exhibition *Mirobolus, Macadam et Cie* he saw at the Galerie René Drouin during his stay in Paris in 1948. For both artists, black literally obscures, confronting the viewer with the void.

Buchi (Holes)

In 1959, when Fontana's work was first becoming well known in Britain, the critic Lawrence Alloway explored the purpose of puncturing the canvas. Alloway wrote in terms that identify a dynamic violence in modernity:

> What is the function of the hole which he has been making since 1949? They are usually learned patterns so that they act as a kind of drawing by negative; like holes in a punched card, like bullet holes in a wall, the holes carry information. The surface as implacably given, the carrier of the message, has been a constituent fact of modern art since Gauguin and Mallarmé. Fontana puts things on the surface: ceramics or patches of canvas: he opens up the surface by punched holes and, more recently, by slashes.[24]

At their simplest, the different series of *concetti spaziali*

Lucio Fontana
Concetto spaziale, 1949–50, *Spatial Concept*
Canvas, 55 × 84.6 cm
Catalogo generale: 49-50 B 4 (see p. 135)
Tate, London

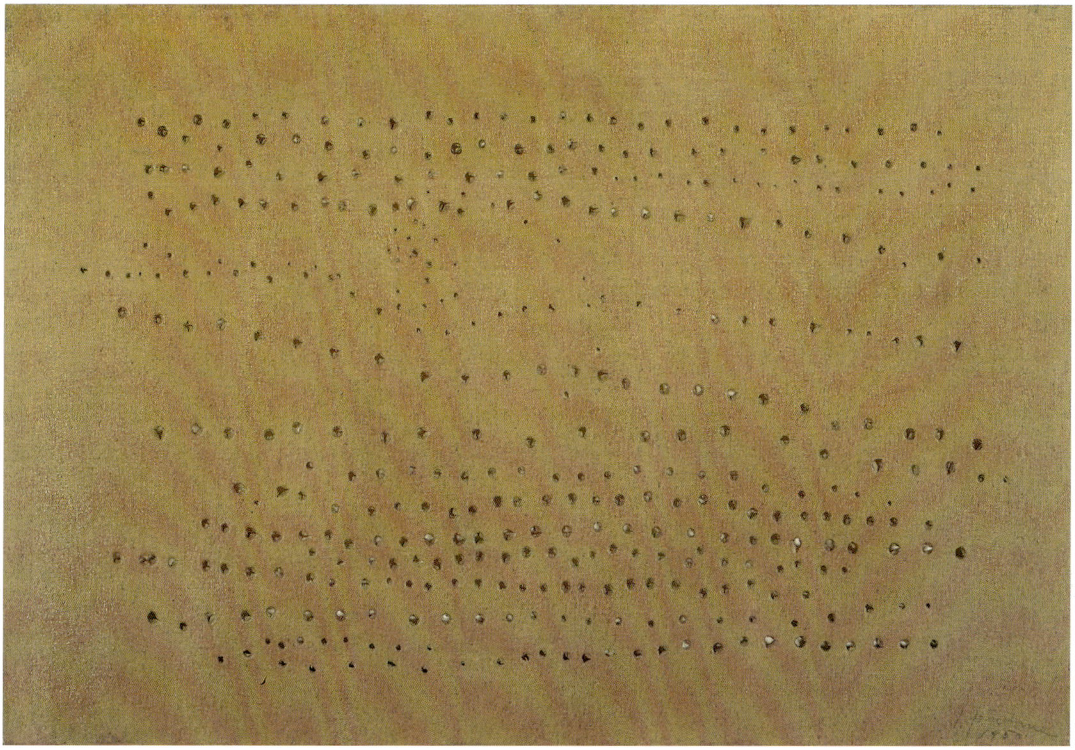

colloquially known as *buchi* (begun in 1949; see p. 71) and *tagli* (begun in 1959; see p. 127), make physical the gesture. The hole is a trace of an action and embodies a memory of an event. In this sense its energy is akin to the use of the canvas as 'an arena in which to act', as Harold Rosenberg famously described contemporary American action painting.[25] The disposition of Fontana's points across the surface evoked Alloway's bullet holes but also, and deliberately, constellations. These associations might act solely in compositional terms were it not for the physical penetration which ensures that Fontana's gesture is multi-dimensional. It cuts through between spaces: from that occupied by the artist (and the viewer), through the fictive space of the canvas, to that which lies beyond. Where realism offered an illusory 'window onto the world', the *buchi* incorporate an actual passing-through to a space that is evocative of infinity. Fontana made this aspiration clear when he spoke of the cosmic qualities of making the *buchi*:

> I make a hole in this canvas, which was the basis of all art and I have created an infinite dimension ... that is precisely the idea, it is a new dimension corresponding with the cosmos. The hole was precisely to create that void at the back. ... Einstein's discovery within the cosmos is of the dimension opening on to the infinite, without an end. So, having already first, second and third [pictorial] planes, what must I do to go beyond? I make a hole in the canvas and the infinite comes through, light comes through, there is no need to paint.[26]

Fontana's spatial dialogue is, therefore, dynamic and its character is determined by the direction of the physical action. He punctured many of the *buchi* from the front, which has the effect of drawing the viewer through the surface and into space. There are several, however, in which the holes erupt from the surface, carrying the force of the gesture towards the viewer in a way that is at once energetic and threatening (see p. 93). The force of these actions has been understood as violent but, at least when considering them in the late 1960s, Fontana emphasised the creative. In the same conversation, he claimed:

> Many people have thought that I was trying to destroy; but that is untrue. I have constructed, not destroyed, that is the key issue.[27]

Through this dynamic bridging of the spatial difference Fontana also implied a temporal dimension. The implication is that the work may encompass a vision onto the future and that the potential is there to pass through to another time and space. The magnitude of this possibility may help to explain Fontana's assertion in 1968: 'My discovery was the hole and that is it: I am content to go to my grave after such a discovery.'[28]

Alberto Burri

Burri is an artist of extraordinary, even alarming, inventiveness. In a period of fifteen years from 1948, he made an unprecedented body of individual, complex and highly wrought works. Setting aside his apprenticeship in painting (to which he came after training as a doctor and serving as a prisoner of war), Burri's personality first came to the fore through his inclusion of unorthodox materials in his paintings, beginning with tar and pumice but famously including sacking (see pp. 77, 79). Weight and age, fragility and neutrality were properties that recurred, and the resulting works deliberately defy painting.

As such, Burri's production of this period may be seen as a negation of the very system that allowed it to be made. The vibrant cultural scene in Italy has been seen as an establishment concession to radicalism while fundamentally conservative political-economic structures were maintained for strategic reasons (circumscribed by the country's position at the heart of the Mediterranean and on the western edge of the Iron Curtain). More acutely, the critic Germano Celant has remarked that it was only through the arts that the harsh reality of the recent Fascist and wartime past could be addressed and repaired.[29] One of the striking characteristics of Burri's work, however, is the violence that it subsumed. This was less through the harnessing of the violent gesture – though this is never far away – and more through a deep-seated turmoil reconciled within the arena of each work but erupting again in the next. His canvases congeal, fragment and bulge (*sacchi* and *gobbi*; see p. 99), and, latterly, are directly attacked (*legni* and *combustioni*; see pp. 100–1, 53–4). In the circumstances of the blossoming welfare of post-war Italy they seem to concentrate a residual tension that would eventually emerge in the social violence and terror of the late 1960s and 1970s.

For his part, Burri rejected interpretation and generally refused to offer any elucidation himself. In a rare statement of 1955, he claimed:

> Words are no help to me when I try to speak about my painting. It is an irreducible presence which refuses to be converted into any other form of expression. It is a presence both imminent and active. This is what it stands for: to exist so as to signify and to exist so as to paint.
>
> My painting is a reality which is a part of myself, a reality that I cannot reveal in words. It would be easier for me to say what does not need to be painted, what does not pertain to painting, what I exclude from my work sometimes with deliberate violence, sometimes with satisfaction.

> Were I master of an exact and less threadbare terminology, were I a marvellous alert and enlightened critic, I still could not verbally establish a close connection with my painting; my words would be marginal notes upon the truth within the canvas. For years pictures have led me, and my work is just a way of stimulating the drive.
>
> I can only say this: painting for me is a freedom attained, constantly consolidated, vigilantly guarded so as to draw from it the power to paint more.[30]

Beyond the trenchant individualism characteristic of the artist lies an urgent intuition. For Burri, painting was 'part of myself' which was also a self-perpetuating drive: 'to exist so as to paint.' The subtext of creative necessity is powerfully present without explaining the accompanying violence, except in reference to exclusion.

Burri is usually described as solitary but self-assured. The critic Milton Gendel observed in 1954: 'In keeping with Burri's air of dedication, the studio is thick-walled, whitewashed, neat and ascetic.'[31] It is tempting to see the works through this isolation, to see the hostility and tension transferred to the astonishingly manipulated surfaces. From the earliest years this bred the equations between Burri's sacking and his medical training. James Johnson Sweeney, in his 1955 monograph on the artist, wrote of 'blood and flesh',[32] and the reddened and torn fabric seems to parallel the staunching of wounds that Burri certainly experienced as a wartime doctor (p. 79). Though this view is persuasive to a degree, the *sacchi* also speak for a wider context of impoverishment or, more accurately, of necessary frugality – the use, patching and reuse of which stretches a material beyond the limits of its function. The sack is patched with other, smaller pieces salvaged from disintegrated remnants (p. 29). Much has, rightly, been made of the contrast between the (implied) wealth of the supplier – often New World countries – and the tattered frugality of the recipients. Gendel remarked at the time that a Milanese collector of contemporary art excluded Burri because he considered the sacks dirty. The artist himself recalled the disapproval voiced by the Communists, who considered the material degrading in another sense, but whom he suspected of acknowledging that it could be a thing of beauty.[33]

This ambiguous position – between political and creative activity – was part of a wider anxiety identified at that moment by the Existentialists. Burri's art may be read as an assertion of the individual freedom to reject idealism, to turn against the comforting certainties of opposition that fed the programme of the Socialist Realism of Renato Guttuso and others (at least up until Stalin's death in 1953), and to express a more troubled sense of being in the world. Indeed, the struggle that Burri undertakes during the 1950s seems to grow more acute and urgent as the decade wears on. Far from assuaging the anxiety apparent in his work through unorthodox materials, he heightens the level of tension by other devices.

The power in Burri's work comes from the vestiges of struggle. The aspect of calm secured in the *bianchi* runs in tandem with the dense exclusiveness of the *neri* and, strikingly, the insistent introduction of red: flat, impassive and strident (see pp. 16, 65, 67). The struggle takes place on the surface, in colour and material. In addition, there is also a subtle layering at work, as Burri plays with the space that can be contained within the structure. The rough surface confronts the viewer with a reality that speaks of the daily grind of poverty. In some senses these works are, therefore, explicitly political in bringing the harsh realities of 1950s Italy into gallery spaces frequented by the better-off.

Beyond this surface lies another, enclosed layer. One of the reasons why the *rossi* have been seen as wounds is because of what they partially conceal; something palpable seems to be held within the *sacchi*, recalling their service as containers but also evocative of that secondary life that they subsequently take on: wiping, absorbing, binding, blocking. Further still lies the board or sheet of material on which the composition is built, a simple foundation layer from which the viewer is largely screened by the upper surfaces.

This furthest layer may be understood in different ways, as if Burri presents the viewer with a glimpse of the reverse of reality; the smooth mount would equate with the public facade, while the tattered interior is a metaphor for the struggle for order taking place within society and each individual. Given the social reality embedded in the rough surface, the unruffled layer may be the equivalent of the social class that could afford to ignore the reality on which it, nevertheless, relies. This is the era in which the migrations of workers from the countryside to the affluent post-war cities – Burri was working in the Rome depicted in the *Ladri di biciclette* (The bicycle thieves, 1948) and *La dolce vita* (1960) – bore with it a widespread disorientation.[34] Psychologically, however, Burri's work seems to invert the established hierarchy and to show the uncertainties that lie behind an individual's outward appearance; the struggle to survive hand-to-mouth stands behind 'la bella figura' – the 'keeping up appearances' of Italian post-war experience.

This interplay became more extreme with Burri's radical adoption of fire. Wood burns, so to adopt a blowtorch as a means of mark-making is, of necessity, an act of premeditated assault. Burri's skill is to conjure from this violence a sense of degradation

Alberto Burri
Sacco e oro, 1953, *Sacking and Gold*
Sacking, oil and gold on canvas, 86 × 101 cm
Catalogo sistematico: 242 (see p. 135)
Isabella del Frate Rayburn, New York

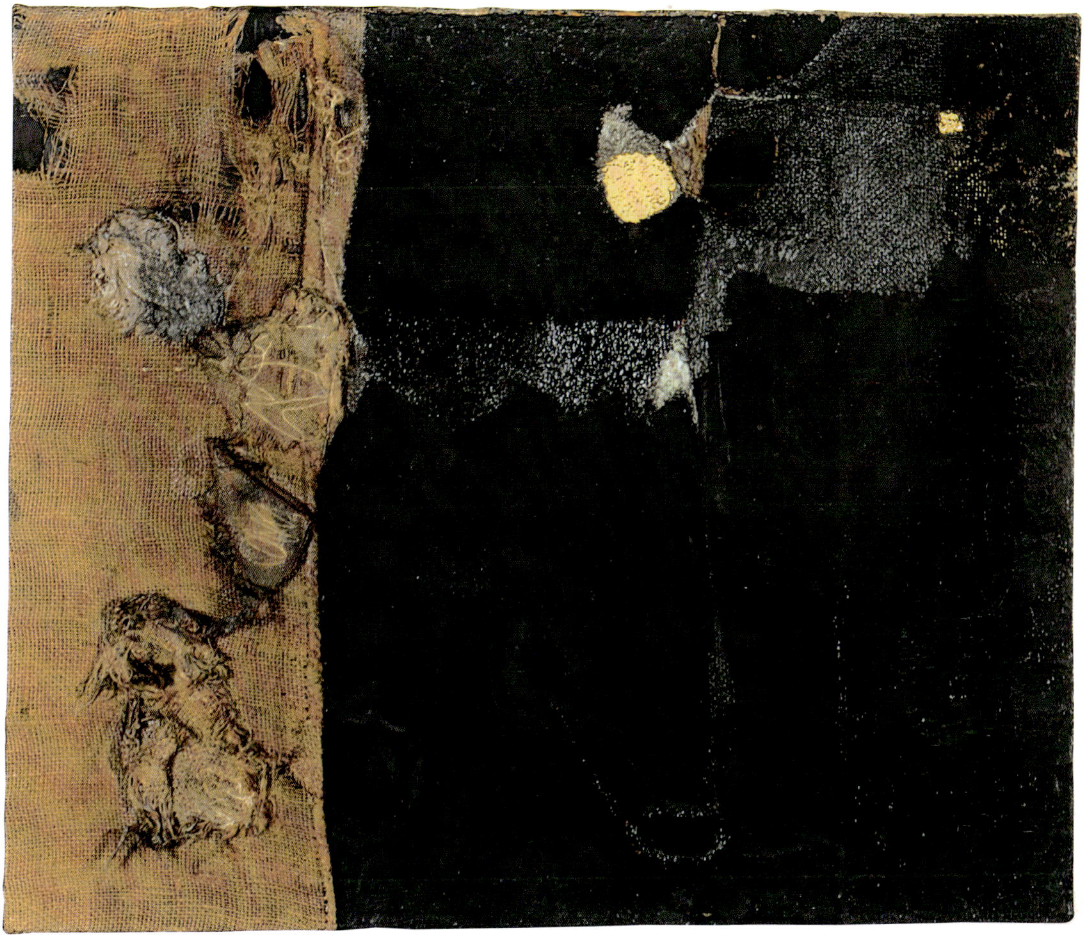

Alberto Burri
Sacco H3, 1954, *Sacking H3*
Sacking, pumice stone, oil paint and Vinavil on canvas, 47 × 59 cm
Catalogo sistematico: 381 (see p. 135)
Fondazione Palazzo Albizzini 'Collezione Burri', Città di Castello

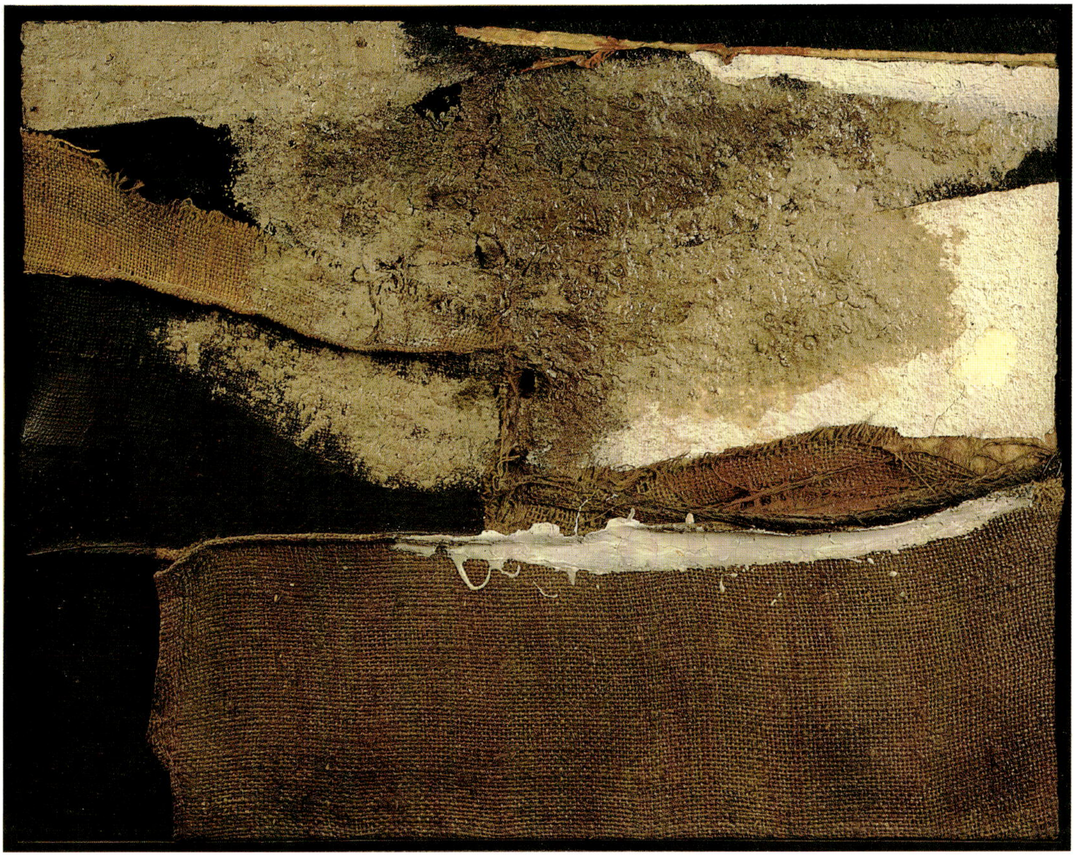

closely allied to that in the *sacchi*. The wood in the *legni* (p. 101), habitually, takes the form of strips of veneer so that the material under attack is precious – the (spoiled) stuff of craftsmanship.

If in these works Burri appears to condense the space between the superficial appearance and the attack that he is making upon it, then this seems to be followed with even more virulence in the opening years of the 1960s. The tension is acute in the burnt *plastiche* (pp. 53–4, 119). There is a searing tragedy in these works. Buckling and retracting as it dragged the fire back into itself, the blackened edges of plastic are disturbingly beautiful. The artist has lavished care on its manipulation but this cannot disguise the violent imagery (what Maurizio Calvesi has called an 'abstract theatre of violence'),[35] comparable to medieval images of the flames of hell. Here Burri seems to confront the void of his own making. This is not the sublime space of Fontana's idealism but something altogether more harrowing. Their power seems to draw upon a deep-seated and urgent anxiety, as they capture a terrible sense of powerlessness and inevitability to man's existence. Whatever the inspiration within or outside the artist himself, the resolution of this particular crisis in Burri's experience is seen in the ensuing *plastiche* on board, where the form is calmer and irrefutably sexual.

CoBrA

CoBrA – taking its name from the first letters of Copenhagen, Brussels and Amsterdam – was established in 1948 as a deliberate break with the pre-war dominance of Paris within the art world. Among the key figures were the Danish artist Asger Jorn, the Dutch painters Karel Appel, Constant, and Corneille, and the Belgian poet Christian Dotremont. Inspired by gestural abstraction and Surrealism, among their central interests were creative and political freedom, spontaneity (born of an appreciation of the art of non-western cultures and the untrained, especially children), and collaborative artwork (involving painters and poets). When the failure of group activity became inevitable in 1951, they disbanded. Jorn, Appel and Corneille (alongside Wifredo Lam) began to visit Albisola in 1954, where they made ceramics alongside Fontana, and were associated with the *Bauhaus Imagginiste*.

Combustioni (Burnings)

Burri began to burn his works in 1954 using a blowtorch to mark paper and, from 1956, to scorch wood in the *legni* series (pp. 100–1). In 1962 he used the same tool, though to radically different effect, in his *plastiche* (pp. 53–4, 119). All these actions combined violence and danger, but under conditions of tight control. They lent a physicality to the production and the result. Like the *sacchi*, the *legni* were the result of an exploration of rejected materials. They differed in the extreme nature of the artist's intervention that established an evident unity through the trace of a single-minded action. Like Fontana's *buchi*, Burri's *combustioni* are witness to an event that approaches Harold Rosenberg's contemporary description of the work as 'an arena in which to act'.[36] The process, however, brings it to the point of what has been called 'painting by subtraction'.[37]

While the *legni* predate related works by other artists, Burri was hardly alone in harnessing fire to a paradoxical shift from destruction to creation. Notable among his contemporaries was Yves Klein, who used a more cumbersome fire-torch to make fire-paintings in the first half of 1961. Interestingly Klein underpinned his activity by reference to Gaston Bachelard's book, *Psychoanalysis of Fire* where the philosopher pinpointed its transformative speed:

> Fire is ... a privileged phenomenon that can explain anything. If all that changes slowly may be explained by life, all that changes quickly is explained by fire. Fire is the ultra-living element. It is intimate and universal.[38]

Burri's *plastiche* (begun in 1962) demonstrate his harnessing of the consuming energy of fire identified by Bachelard. Plastic presented quite different prospects from wood, because of the physical make-up of the material responded in stages prior to conflagration: from malleability, through liquefaction to combustion. Furthermore, depending on his initial choice, Burri found that these stages afforded the potential for a new type of layered transparency. By rending the veils of his materials, Burri appears to open a glimpse into the void which is made all the more apocalyptic through the manipulation of fire.

Concetti spaziali (Spatial concepts)

Until his return to Italy in 1947 Fontana had primarily worked in three dimensions and he carried this approach across to his ensuing canvases by consistently calling each *concetto spaziale*. The use of the generic title – although Fontana himself colloquially used terms such as *buchi* – united his whole output. In 1959 he wrote: 'I call all my paintings spatial concepts [so they are] neither paintings nor sculptures.'[39] Late in life he elaborated:

> From the outset I never called the work I was doing in 1946 painting, I called it a 'spatial concept'. This is because for me

> painting is a matter of ideas ... making a hole was a radical gesture which broke the space of the canvas as if to say: after this we are free to do what we like. The surface cannot be confined within the edges of the canvas, it extends into the surrounding space.[40]

However inspired by scientific endeavour, Fontana never lost sight of the creative impulse. With considerable poetic mystery, he added to each of his *tagli* the term *'attesa'* (p. 126), usually translated as waiting. This evokes the languid passivity of interwar works of this title by Carlo Carrà and Arturo Martini, in which realism and political context combine to suggest a timeless *italianità*.[41] Fontana uses the term to counterpoint such stasis with the action of cutting, introducing the temporal into the spatial. The passivity is contemplative, both for the artist and for the viewer in approaching some understanding of the result. Waiting is at the heart of the inaction in Samuel Beckett's *En attendant Godot* and Eugène Ionesco's *Les Chaises* (Waiting for Godot and The chairs, both of 1952), where it bears a sense of a futile occupancy of time. Fontana's position was more positive: his sense of waiting is one of expectancy that will be fulfilled rather than expectation that will not.

The Corporeal

One of Manzoni's many, and ironic, challenges to perpetuity is found in his pneumatic works begun in 1959. He prepared balloons and bases which the purchaser could acquire as *corpo d'aria* (Body of air), or could 'buy my breath too' by having Manzoni blow-up the balloon to make a *fiato d'artista* (The artist's breath).[42] The sealed balloon was briefly anchored to, rather than supported by, its base until its permeability made disintegration inevitable.

Such personalised gestures increasingly focused on Manzoni's own body in the final years of his short life. In two events in 1960, he marked hard-boiled eggs with his thumbprint by way of a signature, before they were consumed. Most extreme was the *Merda d'artista* (Artist's shit), which he described impassively:

> In the month of May '61 I produced and tinned 90 tins of 'artist's shit' (30 grammes each) naturally preserved (made in Italy). A previous project had been to produce phails of 'artist's blood'.[43]

Defiant of social conventions and the commercialisation of art, Manzoni's gestures were provocations. His colleague Ettore Sordini recently declared: 'he [Manzoni] did not regard them as a creative act. It was in the tradition of Milanese mockery.'[44] Beyond the outrage, however, lies a simple but moving meditation upon the ephemeral nature of existence and the mortality of the body.

Cotone (Cottons)

In extending the reach of the *achromes* in 1960 Manzoni adopted a variety of materials that were inherently white and thus fulfilled the requirement of neutrality. Cotton was one of these as he aligned square pads, wads or cottonwool balls (p. 87). Just as with the kaolin *achromes*, cotton afforded subliminal medical associations. His contemporary use of man-made materials provides a contrast to the *cotone*.

Dada and Surrealism

More a loose chain of groups than a movement, Dada was officially named in neutral wartime Zurich, in 1917, by the poets Hugo Ball and Tristan Tzara. Their outrage against the destruction of the First World War, that they saw as brought about by western industrial capitalism, was shared by a wide variety of artists, and there were parallel developments in Barcelona, New York (around Marcel Duchamp), Berlin, Paris and elsewhere. The resulting work has been seen as an art of negation, an anti-art. In Paris in the 1920s Surrealism emerged as a more programmatic delving into the unconscious, and at the expense of Dada's collapse. After the Second World War, the reputations of Dada and its artists and poets – including Kurt Schwitters (not strictly Dada), Tzara and Duchamp – were revived, especially among other artists. Duchamp's 'readymades', manufactured objects presented as works of art simply through the artist's choice, began to have an impact as seminal provocations. In Italy, where both Dada and Surrealism had been suppressed under Fascism, the Milanese Galleria Schwarz fed a thirst for Dada's anarchic and paradoxical irony. Tzara, E.L.T. Mesens, Duchamp and others visited the *Tenth International Surrealist Exhibition* (held there in 1961) and, in 1964, Schwarz issued an edition of Duchamp's readymades.

Existentialism

In the 1940s, the French Existential writers Jean-Paul Sartre, Albert Camus, Maurice Merleau-Ponty and others identified the impossibility of human communication and the consequences for public (and political) life. The futility of existence – whether through the collapse or the exercise of an individual's will (in Sartre's *La Nausée* (Nausea) and Camus's *L'Etranger* (The Outsider) respectively)[45] – was recognised by a generation suspicious of the attempted return of the established pre-war culture. Burri's attitude has been seen in terms of a 'Camusian *révolte*' and described as a refusal 'to collaborate with a system that ... failed to guarantee the physical and moral integrity of man'.[46] Certainly, the Existential suspicion of the pointlessness of

Lucio Fontana
Concetto spaziale, 1960, *Spatial Concept*
Oil on canvas, 81 × 100 cm
Catalogo generale: 60 O 8 (see p. 135)
Fondazione Lucio Fontana, Milan

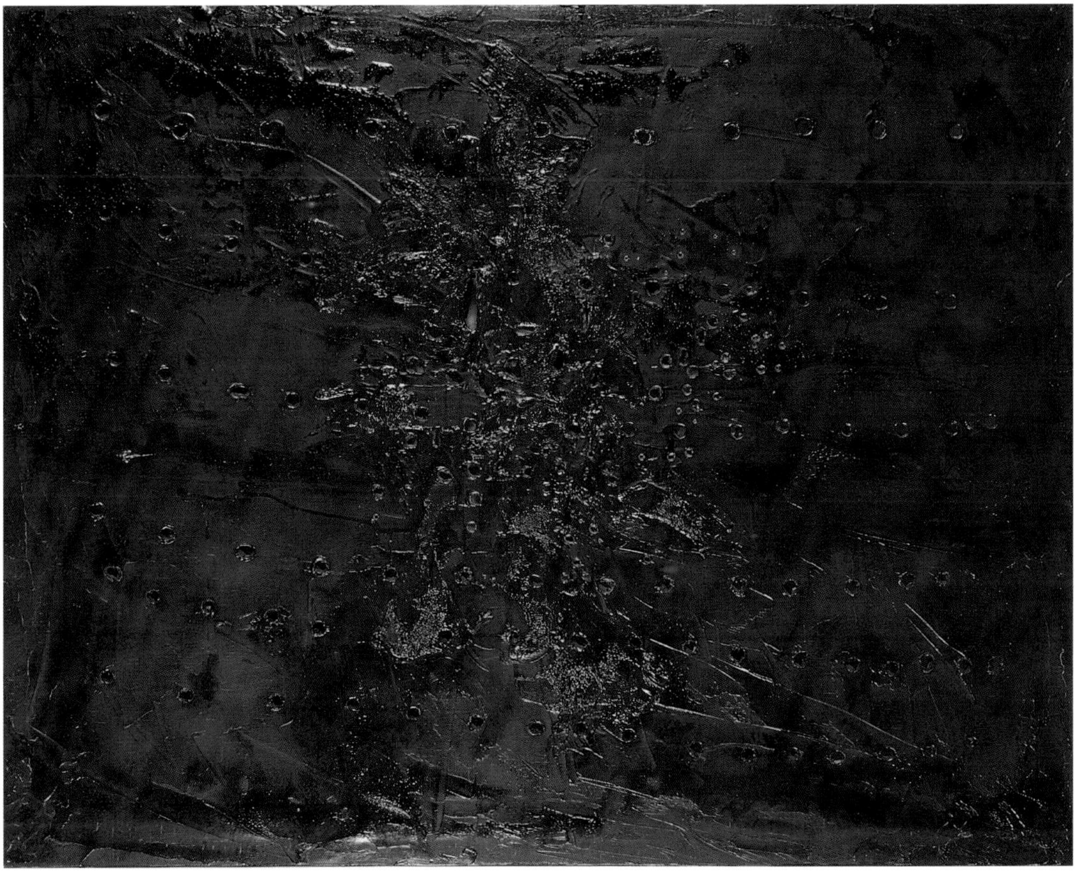

Piero Manzoni
Achrome, 1960
Cotton, 64 × 49 cm
Catalogo generale: 727 (see p. 135)
Archivio Piero Manzoni, Milan

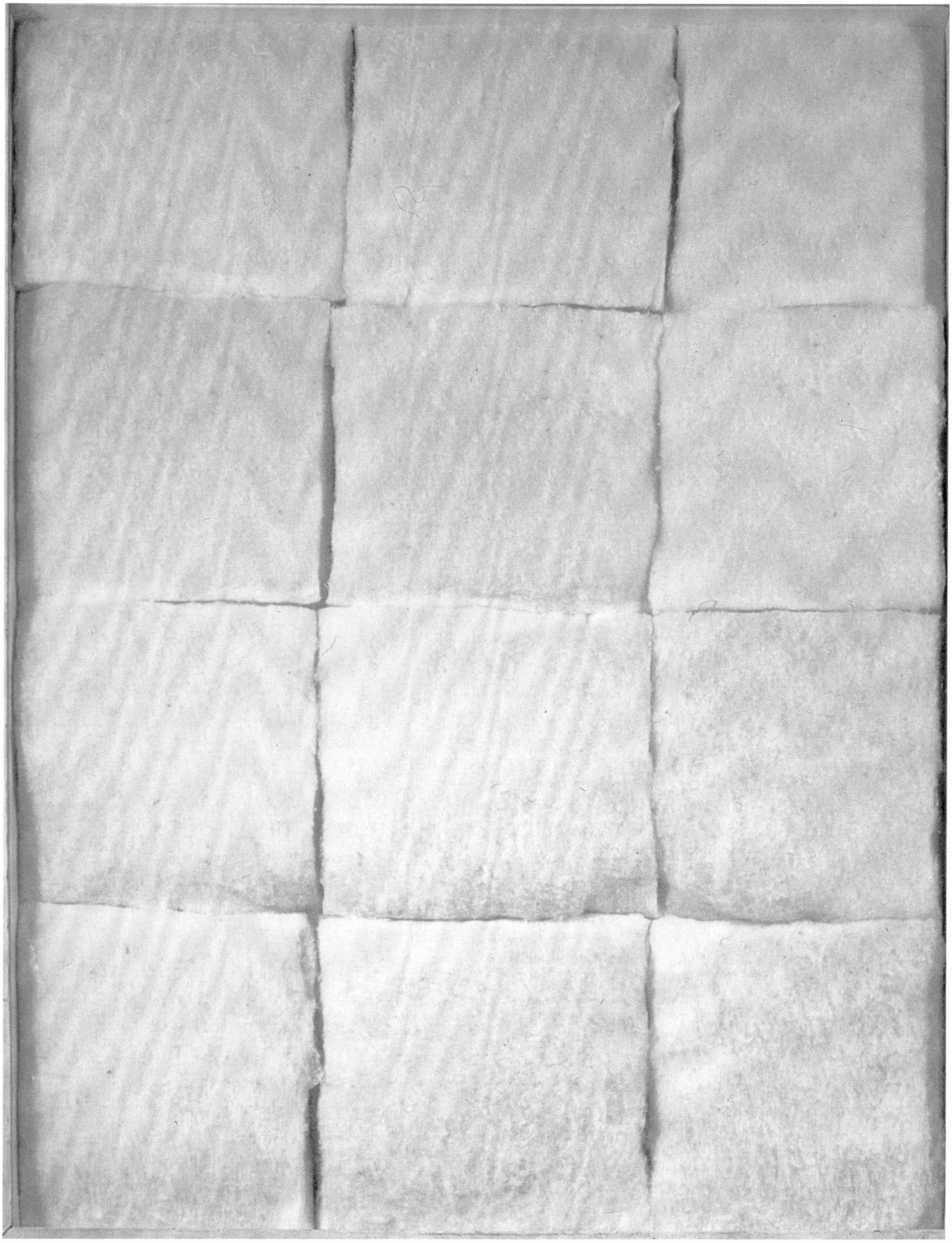

communication especially concerned artists, confronting them with mute existence or a defiant exploration of individual concerns.

For some, Merleau-Ponty's *La Phénoménologie de la perception* (The phenomenology of perception) provided a means for taking artistic practice beyond Existentialism. Although he famously identified the 'doubt' embedded in Cézanne's practice, his exploration of the perceptual relationship between consciousness and what he termed 'being in the world' was most significant. As works of art are seen as acting on the viewer phenomenologically – having an appreciable effect on the physical experience of the individual – so the emphasis of Burri and Fontana (and others) on material texture and spatial effect may gain in resonance. Exploring the nature of meaning, Merleau-Ponty explained that, irrespective of the apparent role of chance, 'facts in their multiplicity coalesce and show up a certain way of taking a stand in relation to the human situation, reveal in fact an *event* which has its definite outline'.[47] Such an *event* appears to anticipate the action in the work of Burri and Fontana – especially the *plastiche* and *tagli* respectively. In his last work, *L'Œil et l'esprit* (Eye and mind) written in 1960–1, Merleau-Ponty specifically addressed the visible and the artistic. Citing Paul Klee, he wrote:

> There is that which reaches the eye directly, the frontal properties of the visible; but there is also that which reaches it from below – the profound postural latency where the body raises itself to see – and that which reaches vision from above like the phenomenon of flight, of swimming, of movement, where it participates no longer in the heaviness of origins but in free accomplishments. Through it, then, the painter touches the two extremities. In the immemorial depth of the visible, something moved, caught fire, and engulfed his body; everything he paints is in answer to this incitement, and his hand is 'nothing but the instrument of a distant will'.[48]

Ferri (Irons)

In response to Maurizio Calvesi's 'tense questions on the meaning of the sacks or the iron' in 1958, Burri 'repeatedly informed me that the material was nothing other than the equivalent of the paint'.[49] He had made the shift to sheet iron in the previous year (see pp. 90–1). The cutting, buckling and welding of the thin metal afforded maximum flexibility while announcing its materiality. Of his use of materials Burri stated:

> What I have sought to draw out of them is only their property. Iron, for example, suggested a sense of hardness, weight, sharpness. I was not interested in 'representing' iron. It was

immediately obvious that the material was iron. I wanted instead to explain what iron was capable of.[50]

Many of the works are reminiscent of armoured vehicles even if Burri avoided the explicit associations exploited by his colleague Ettore Colla or the French artist César, who both salvaged wartime scrap-metal for their sculptures. The roughness in Burri's *ferri* is found in the welded seams and the colour changes resulting from heating, so that they parallel the active interventions of the *combustioni* rather than the decay of the *sacchi*.

Lucio Fontana

Born into an Italian–Argentinian family in Rosario de Santa Fe, Argentina, in 1898, Lucio Fontana spent sustained periods in both countries and had a long-established career before the Second World War. His work has many parallel strands. The monumental statuary of his youth developed through official commissions to the residual figuration of his immediate post-war works. The turbulent material of the clay sculptures made at Albisola in the 1930s may be linked to the *nature* made there twenty years later. At the same time, his engagement with the abstraction associated with the Galleria Il Milione around 1933–5, can been seen as the seedbed of his reductive means in the 1950s. He returned to Italy in 1947, fresh from teaching at the Academia de Bellas Artes in Buenos Aires and the more radical Altamira Academy. Under Fontana's guidance, some of the students extended the exploration of Constructivism and published the *Manifiesto blanco* (White manifesto) in 1946, in which the programme of *Spazialismo* is first laid out. The manifesto concludes:

> Thousands of years have passed in artistic–analytical development, the moment of synthesis arises ... We conceive of this synthesis as an addition of physical elements: colour, sound, movement, time, space, integrating a physical–psychical unity. Colour (the element of space), sound (the element of time), and motion (that develops in time and space) are the fundamental forms of the new art which comprehends the four dimensions of existence, time and space.
> The new art demands the functioning of all the energies of man in creation and interpretation. The Being manifests itself integrally, with the plenitude of its vitality.[51]

Fontana and *Spazialismo* were intertwined. He was the prime-mover of this idealistic revision of the purposes of cultural activity. Although he is most closely associated with the development of the movement on his arrival in Milan, it is clear that he considered this a continuation of the activities in Argentina.[52]

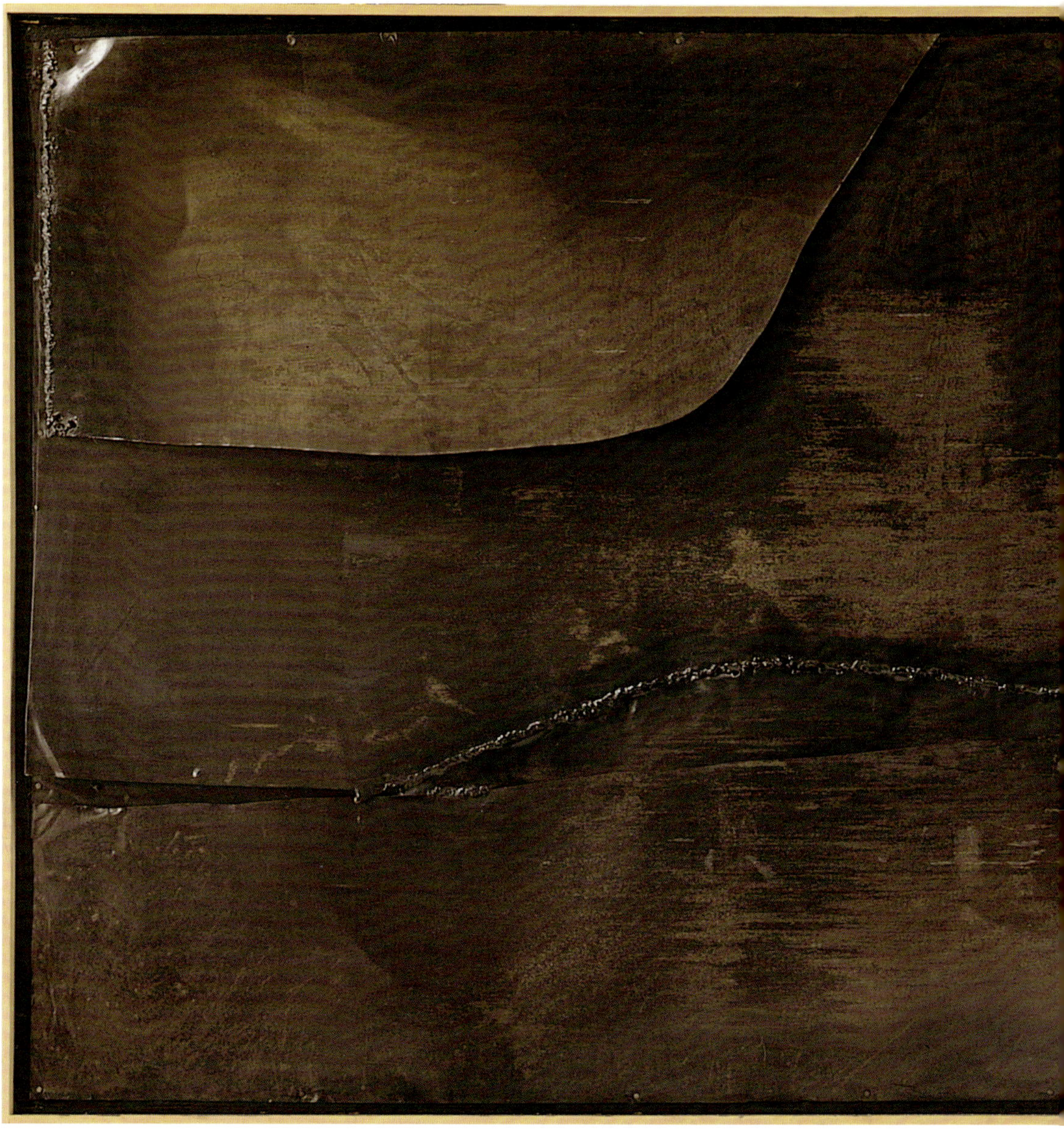

Alberto Burri
Ferro SP1, 1958, *Iron SP1*
Iron on wood stretcher, 103 × 200 cm
Catalogo sistematico: 664 (see p. 135)
Fondazione Palazzo Albizzini 'Collezione Burri', Città di Castello

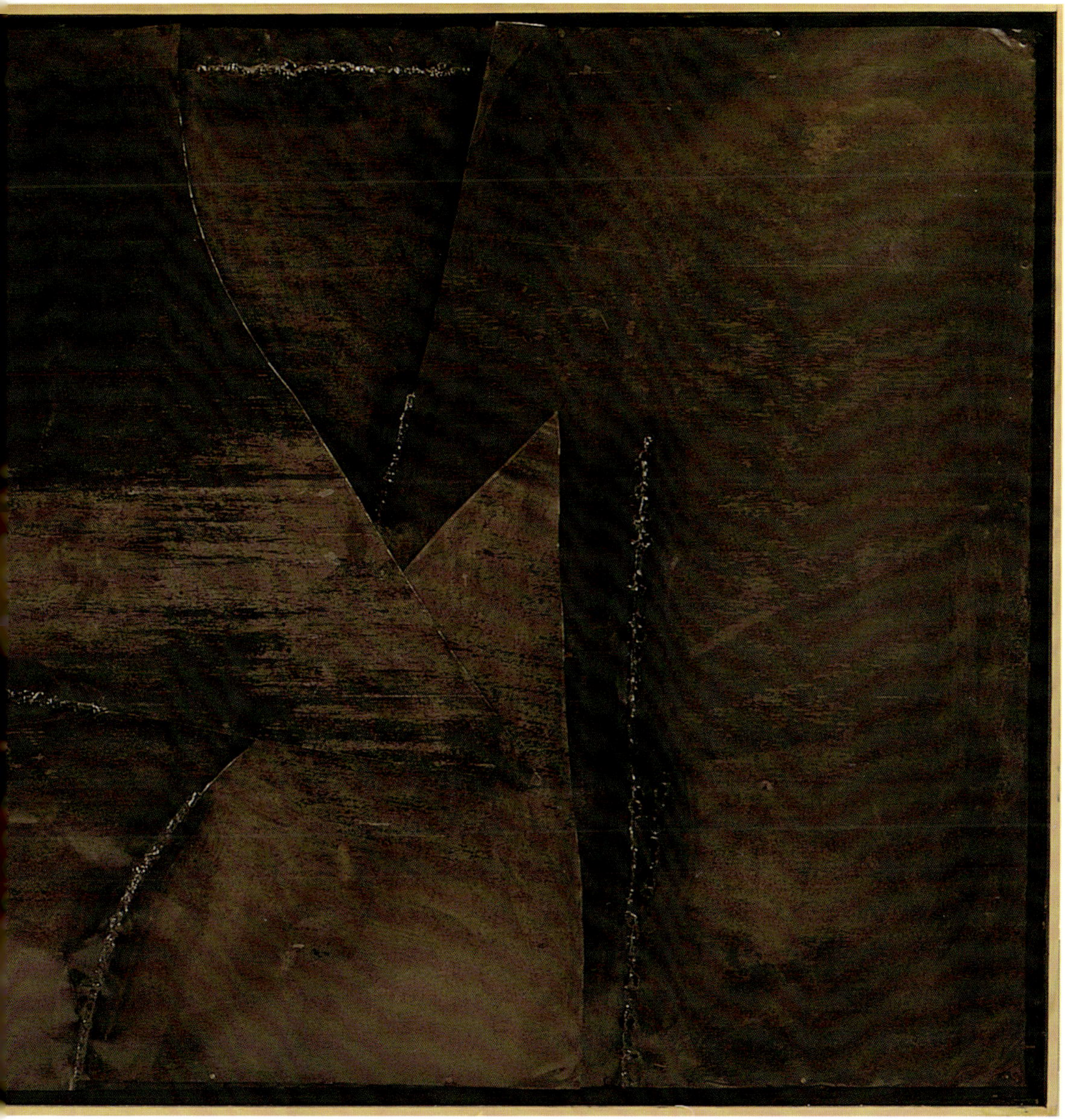

Lucio Fontana
Concetto spaziale, 1960, *Spatial Concept*
Oil on canvas, 100 × 81 cm
Catalogo generale: 60 O 36 (see p. 135)
Private collection

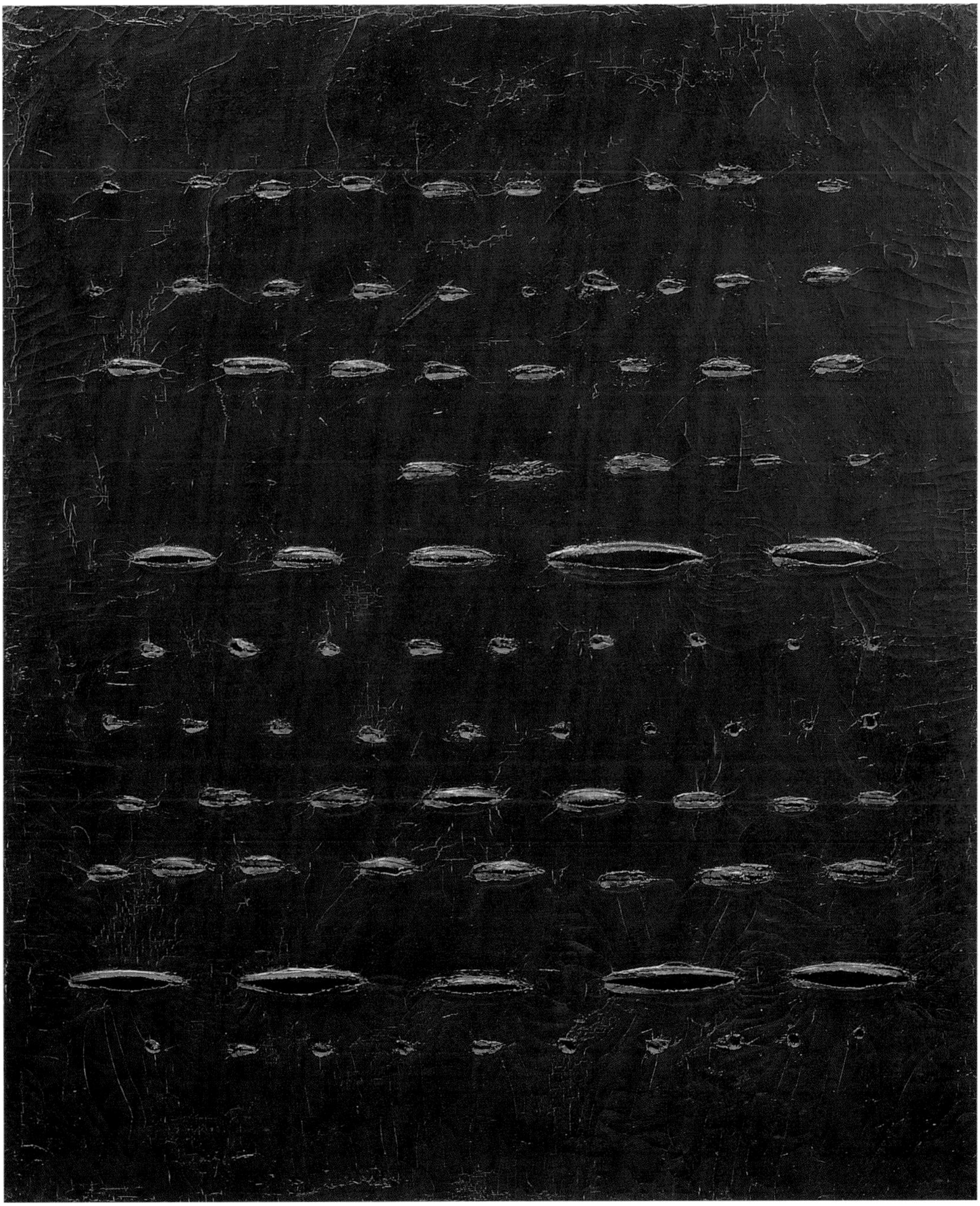

Futurism' published on the front page of the French newspaper *Le Figaro*. The dynamism of Futurism set out to challenge both the complacent culture of Giolittian Italy and the dominance of Parisian modernism. Gathering poets and artists to the cause – including Umberto Boccioni (whose status was only enhanced by his early death in 1916), Giacomo Balla, Carlo Carrà, Luigi Russolo, and Gino Severini – Marinetti created an Italian avant-garde. They accepted modernity and technology, experimented across all arts and with politics and, under Marinetti's continuing guidance, endured as a powerful cultural force through subsequent generations under Fascism. Despite the legacy of this engagement, there was a renewed interest in Futurist abstraction among the young generation of artists after the Second World War; Severini and Balla had exhibitions in Rome and Enrico Prampolini was a key figure in the avant-garde Art Club. On a conceptual level, Fontana cited Boccioni's theoretical position – especially that in the *Manifesto tecnico della scultura futurista* (Technical manifesto of Futurist sculpture) – as a major influence on *Spazialismo*. He observed in 1951:

> Boccioni's manifesto and the [sculpture] Development of a Bottle in Space revolutionised the concept of art: plastic dynamism in space.
> The lessons of Boccioni still inspire Italians; the evolution of the means of art cannot become a new art without new techniques, just as cement revolutionised the aesthetic and the structure of architecture.[57]

Gobbi (Hunchbacks)

In 1954, the Rome-based American critic Milton Gendel interviewed Burri and, rather surprisingly, observed him at work:

> Though Burri may unexpectedly reinforce an associative link by speaking of *Rosso I*, 1954 as a *Gobbo rosso*, or 'Red Hunchback', on the whole he considers that the manifest content of his painting must take care of itself; he is a painter, a solitary, a hunter, who eschews conjecture on his unconscious processes: 'The words don't mean anything to me; they talk around the picture. What I have to express appears in the picture. In this one I have worked with a big red space that is expanding forward and in all directions. With the elements it is involved in a whole chain of pulls and tensions. But this is only the architectonic structure. For the rest I have nothing to add.'[58]

Gendel was quick to identify the 'associative link' that accompanies Burri's use of *gobbo* (hunchback) as a title (p. 99). It is an unusual choice, as most of the series bear the name of materials or colours. The bulges that determine the smooth relief (created by a bent wire fixed between the stretcher and the canvas) are evocative of the physical distortion commonly associated with hunchbacks. Beyond that, however, lie caricatures found in folk and fairy tales. Coincidentally Hannah Arendt recalled these in titling part of her introduction to Walter Benjamin's *Illuminations* 'The Hunchback', explaining the writer's fear of and compassion for a childhood bogeyman to whom childish accidents are attributed.[59]

Greenwich meridian

Manzoni wrote in 1962 of his production of *linee* (lines), drawn on rolls of paper and parcelled up in tubes:

> At the beginning of 1959 I carried out my first lines, at first short, then longer and longer (19.11m, 33m, 63m, 1000 etc.): the longest one I have done to date is 7200m (1960 Herning, Denmark). All these lines are placed in sealed containers. I would also like to draw a white line around the entire Greenwich Meridian![60]

When asked why the lines were so different, Manzoni replied: 'I sell ideas. Ideas with small variations.'[61]

Gutaï

The Japanese painter and writer Jirō Yoshihara founded *Gutaï* (Concreteness) in Ashiya near Osaka in 1954. Based on a rejection of the formalism of both traditional Japanese and imported Western art, *Gutaï* artists – including Shōzō Shimamoto, Kazuo Shiraga and Saburō Murakami – enacted performances and produced works which bore witness to direct physical action. Shimamoto began to puncture his canvases in 1950, at the same time as, but unaware of Fontana's *buchi*; on discovering the coincidence and, believing that his obscurity would count against him, he abandoned the method. It has been argued that, in the light of the persistent American presence even after the 1951 Security Treaty nominally re-established post-occupation independence, such *Gutaï* actions identified the canvas as a site of oppressive western tradition to be rejected.[62]

Yoshihara's manifesto was published in the periodical *Gijutsu-Shicho* in 1956. In the following year, the French painter Georges Mathieu and the critic Michel Tapié visited Japan and initiated important contacts for *Gutaï* in Europe. Fontana contributed to an international survey exhibition, *International Art of a New Era: Informel and Gutaï*, in Osaka in 1958, and by 1960 Manzoni was contributing articles to *Gijutsu-Shicho* and he and Castellani were discussed in *Mizue*.

Alberto Burri
Gobbo bianco, 1953, *White Hunchback*
Cloth, oil, sawdust and pumice stone on canvas, 100 × 86 cm
Catalogo sistematico: 415 (see p. 135)
Fondazione Palazzo Albizzini 'Collezione Burri', Città di Castello

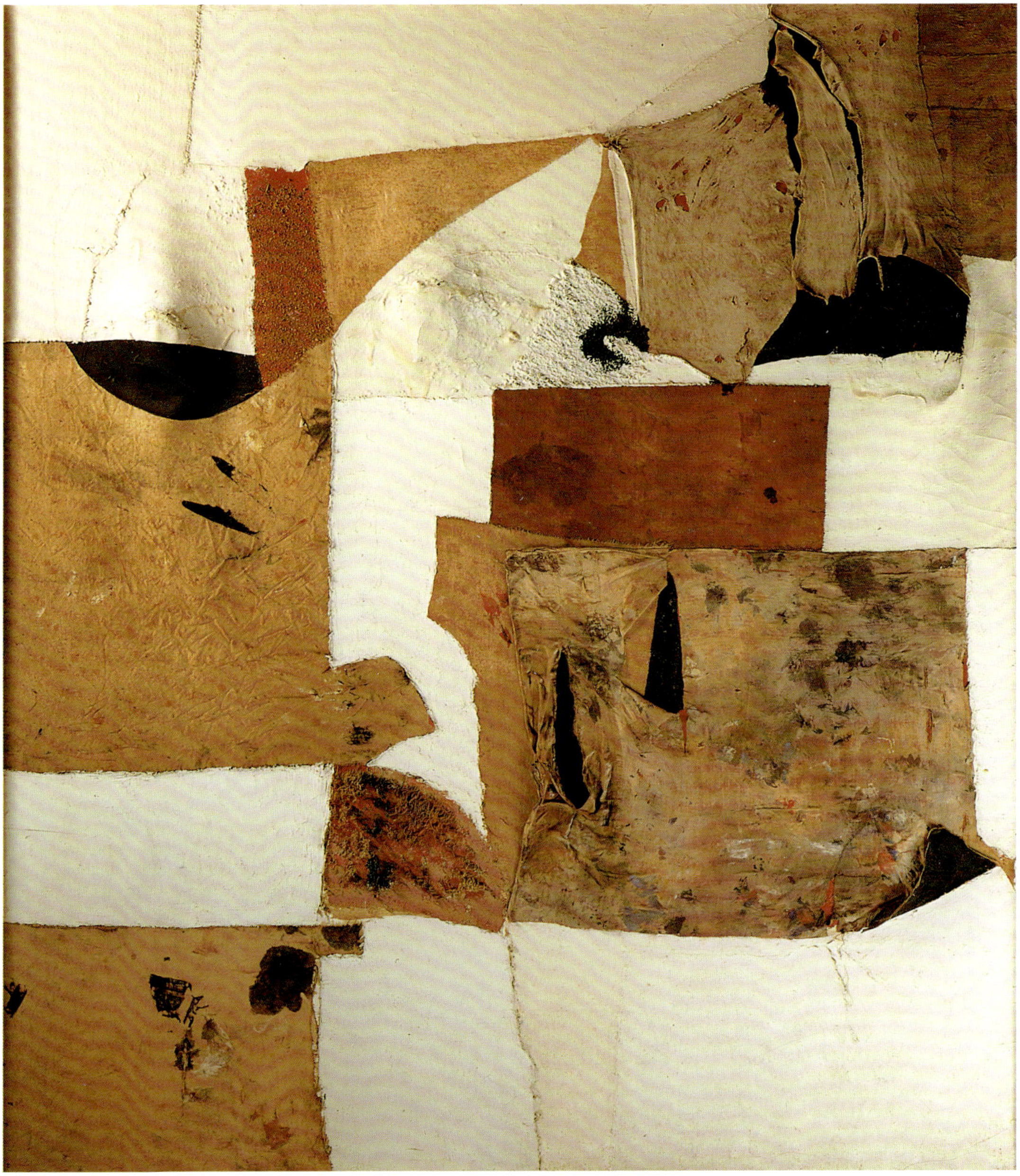

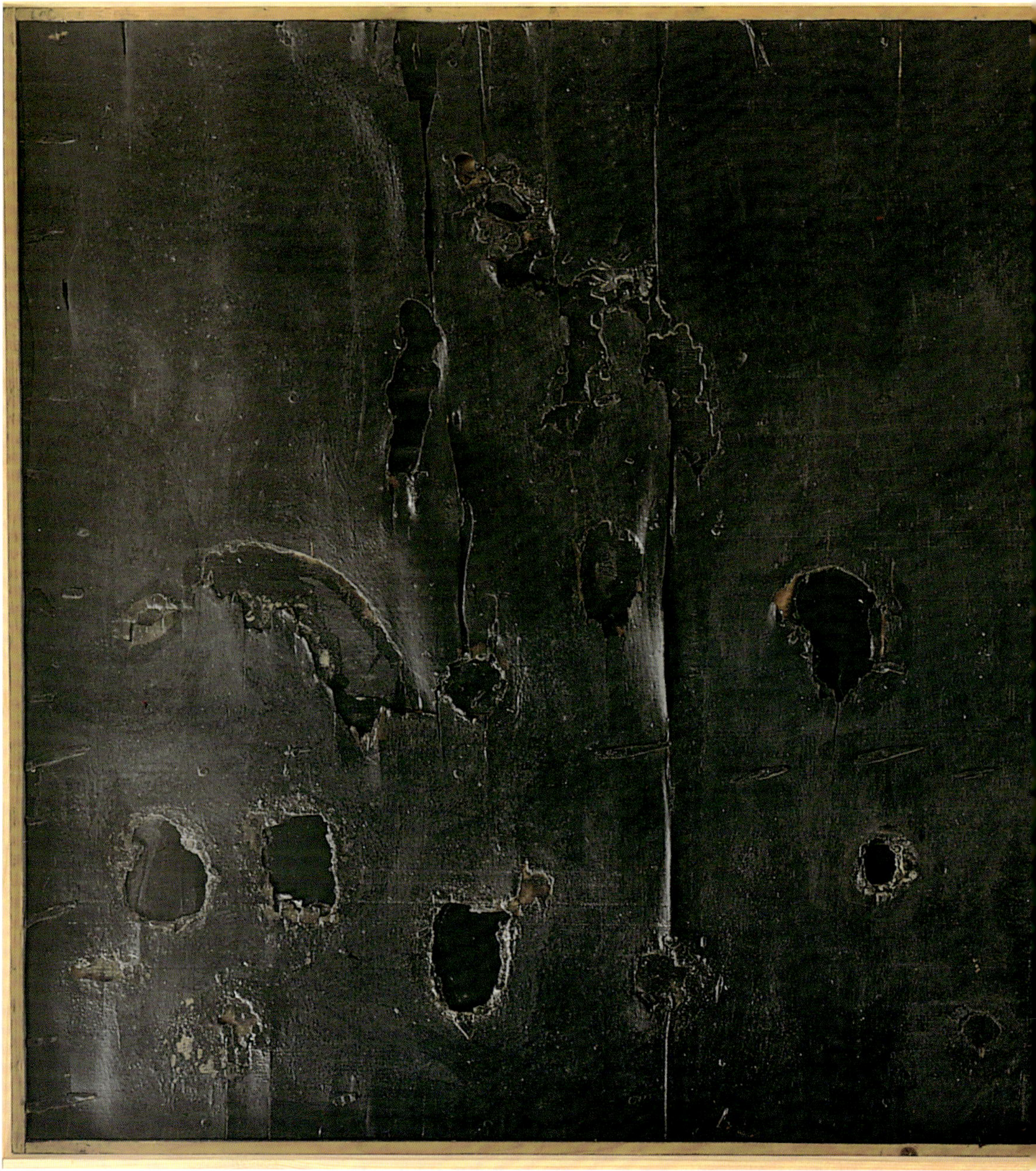

Alberto Burri
Combustione legno, 1955, *Wood Combustion*
Wood, Vinavil and combustion on canvas, 86 × 157 cm
Catalogo sistematico: 583 (see p. 135)
Fondazione Palazzo Albizzini 'Collezione Burri', Città di Castello

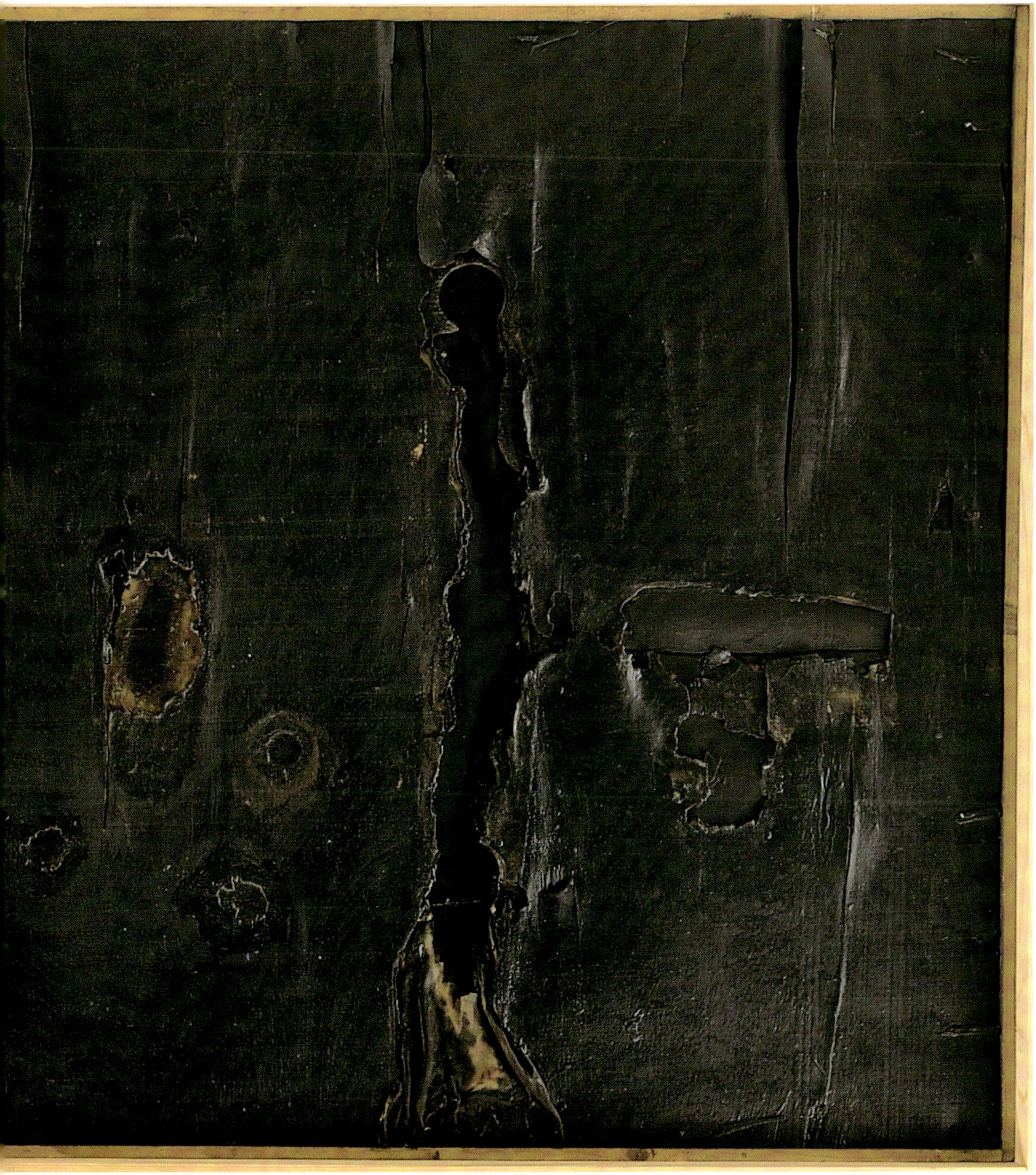

Informel, Tachisme and Astratto-Concretto

A variety of terms used for gestural abstraction have tended to coalesce with time, but *Informel, Tachisme*, and *Astratto-Concretto* originally had specific connotations. All have parallels with the transatlantic trends of Action Painting and Abstract Expressionism and while any claim to causative relationships remains problematic, it is clear that events such as Peggy Guggenheim's display of Jackson Pollock at the 1948 Venice Biennale and his Rome retrospective ten years later had an impact.

The French term *Tachisme* (from 'tache', mark) specifically designated mark-making, and artists as diverse as Georges Mathieu and Hans Hartung, even Nicolas de Staël, were associated with the tendency at various times. A post-Cubist abstraction emerged in Italy with the *Gruppo degli Otto* at Venice in 1952 (featuring, among others, Afro Basaldella and Renato Birolli), subsequently promoted by the critic Lionello Venturi as *Astratto-Concretto*. Although Emilio Vedova was initially included in this group, his work was based in the expressive gesture and he, Burri and Fontana were regarded as 'genuine Italian *Informel*' artists.[63] The same may be said of many of the artists associated with *Arte Nucleare* as they strove to abandon conventional styles. The materiality of their work certainly has parallels with those artists in France to whom Michel Tapié applied the term *Informel* in his book *Un Art autre* (1952): Jean Dubuffet, Jean Fautrier and Wols.

Of the French artists, Dubuffet proved the most versatile and influential. He championed the work of untrained artists (for which he coined the term *Art Brut*), and made a succession of extraordinarily inventive series in the late 1940s and 1950s using unorthodox materials and methods, from incised tar and heavy emulsions of his own invention, to butterfly wings. The viscous blackness of Dubuffet's tar works specifically attracted Burri on his visit to Paris in 1948, and later inspired Manzoni. More generally, Dubuffet's continual reinvention proved exemplary.

Legni (Woods)

When Burri began to scorch wood in 1956, his method remained deliberately pictorial, with the material serving as the canvas for his action (pp. 100–1). His achievement was a dexterous control of the unusual process, so that fire inflects rather than overcomes the material. It has been said that the strips of wood in the *legni* recall the crude palisades of simple dwellings and that they reflect the deprivation that seems to underlie the earlier *sacchi*.[64] However persuasive this argument appears, it should be recognised Burri actually used veneer. This has quite different associations: with craftsmanship rather than subsistence. As a result, the scorching of the material also bears different meanings, for it suggests a degradation and destruction of a certain strand of culture – one that is as superficial as the veneer.

Liberty

> Why shouldn't this receptacle be emptied? Why shouldn't this surface be freed? Why not seek to discover the unlimited meaning of total space, of pure and absolute light?[65]

Manzoni came close to Fontana's cosmic liberation, when he wrote these lines in his text 'Libera dimensione' (Free dimension). Art at the time – a post-war and Cold War era – was circumscribed by a rhetoric of liberty. Individual freedom, the point of Existential debate, became the point of ideological contention with the communist East, so that political support (overt or covert) was a significant element in cultural development in the capitalist West. This may provide a context for Burri's fiercely isolationist attitude: 'painting for me is a freedom attained.'[66]

Piero Manzoni

It is in his responses to contemporary practice that Manzoni marked out his individuality at the end of the 1950s. His position was at once synthetic and oppositional, as he absorbed, explored and subverted the practices that had quickly come to denote Milanese and European avant-gardism. Like many artists working in the turbulent and stimulating atmosphere in 1950s Europe, Manzoni responded to the explorations associated with *Informel*. However, perhaps because he was considerably younger and passed rapidly through the pre-established structures of contemporary practice, he was also quick to reject what he saw as a misguided quasi-mystical admiration for artistic style. Already in his earliest exhibited and published works around 1955–6, Manzoni's response was manifested in off-prints from found objects (pliers, pins), together with the curious 'hominids' (schematic figures) that reflect an immersion in Jungian thought. Like Yves Klein and Burri (whose overlapping exhibitions in Milan in January 1957 affected him profoundly), he experimented with materiality – but it was Fontana's exemplary radicalism that he found most inspiring.

During 1957–8 Manzoni allied himself to the resurgent *Arte nucleare* of Enrico Baj and Sergio Dangelo. He signed various manifestos – notably the *Manifesto contro lo stile* (Manifesto

Piero Manzoni
Achrome, 1958
Kaolin on canvas, 100.3 × 100.3 cm
Catalogo generale: 303 (see p. 135)
Tate, London

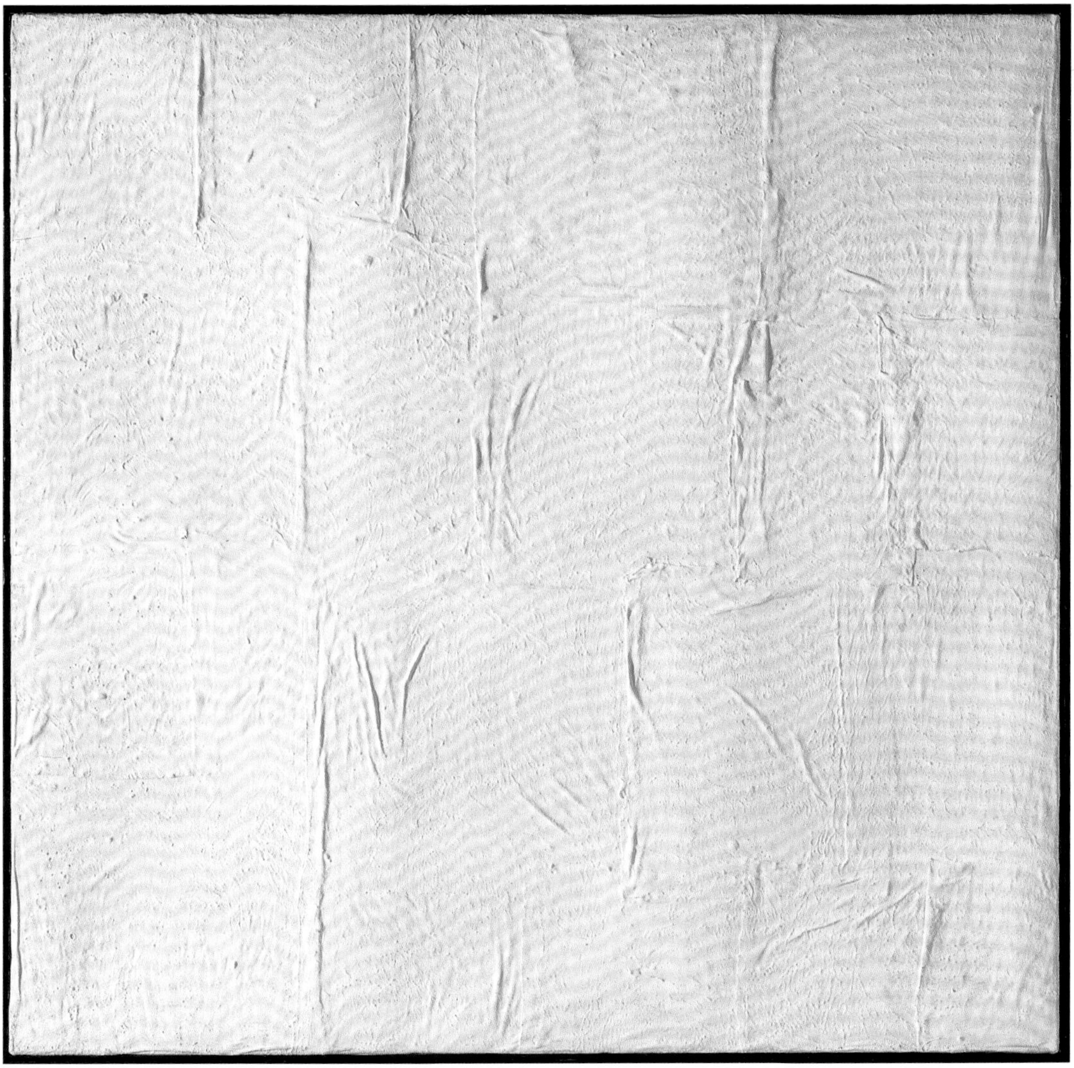

Piero Manzoni
Achrome, 1962
Stones and kaolin on canvas, 100 × 80 cm
Catalogo generale: 1048 (see p. 135)
Archivio Piero Manzoni, Milan

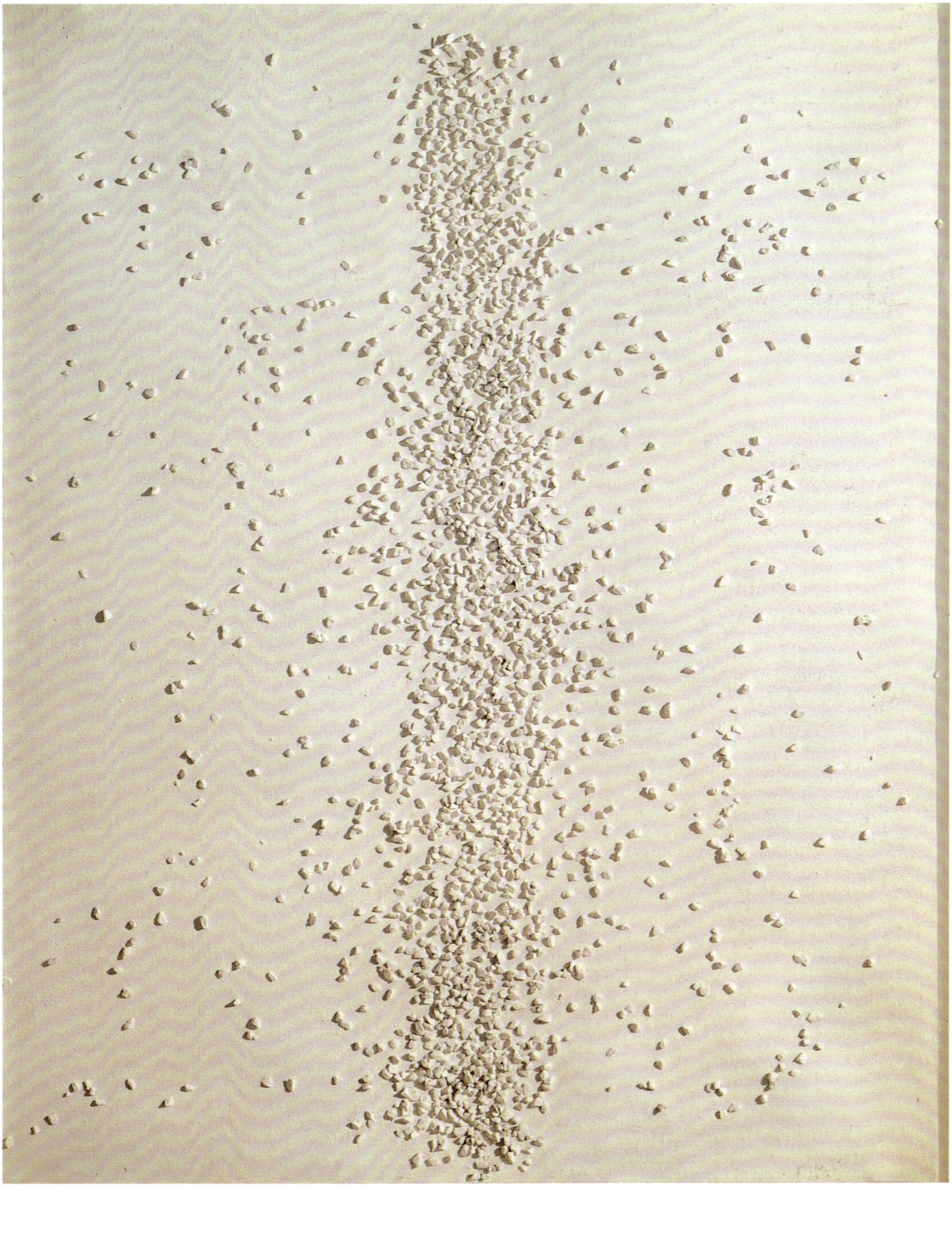

against style) of September 1957 – and in early 1958 shared a three-man show in Bergamo with Fontana and Baj. He was still only twenty-five but, as he proudly declared to a friend: 'I am a kind of symbol of the union of the three initiators of the three avant-garde movements in Milan.'[67]

At this moment he was in the process of shedding the last figurative references before the development of the *achromes*. For Manzoni the fundamental step away from the expressive brushstroke and utopian modernism was towards the absence of colour. The densely white *achromes* embody the liberation of style demanded in the 1957 manifesto. They stretched the confines of the canvas, where the weight of kaolin caused ridging, folding and wrinkling (p. 59). In 'Libera dimensione' (Free dimension) of 1960,[68] he was dismissive of the elaborate resolution of painting, mocking the contemplative passage of the artist backwards and forwards from the easel. By draining the work of colour, he professed, a simple neutrality was possible.

The autonomy and growing three-dimensionality of the *achromes* also marked Manzoni's own independence from *Arte nucleare* (although he co-edited the third issue of their periodical *Il gesto* in 1958). He began exhibiting with Enrico Castellani and Agostino Bonalumi, and formed contacts with the *Zero* group in Germany and the Netherlands. In a second sequence of *achromes* the hand of the artist became increasingly distant, as the repetition and accumulation of material and the unexpected phenomenological aspects of certain substances – the phosphorescent cotton works, the intangible lack of structure of the fibreglass *nuvole* (clouds; p. 115) – expand the viewers' experience. A desire to maintain a high public profile and their international contacts, led Manzoni and Castellani to found the periodical *Azimuth* and associated gallery in 1959. The internationalism was evident in the periodical (which illustrated key works such as Jasper Johns's *Target with Plaster Casts*, 1955) and in Manzoni's increased activities abroad, most notably in his extended stays at Herning in Denmark. There he made his extraordinary *Base del mondo* (Base of the world), 1961, a metre cube of iron to which the title is affixed upside down, so as to imply that it supports the planet.

Manzoni's practice around 1960 moved rapidly towards the dramatic gesture, bordering on performance. The production of works – *linee* (lines inscribed on rolls of paper), *uova* (thumbprinted eggs) – was witnessed by an audience and recorded for posterity. With deliberate echoes of Yves Klein's actions, he notoriously signed people at his 1961 exhibition at Galleria La Tartaruga in Rome, thus designating them as *Sculture viventi* (Living sculptures). In the combination of provocation and ironic distance, Manzoni may be regarded as one of the most significant critics of the materiality of the 1950s. Even the *achromes*, however indebted to the example of Fontana and Burri, may be considered as a comment upon their achievements. A new Duchampian playfulness inflected his work and, with his explicit abandonment of the canvas for the residual object, Manzoni's approach anticipates that of artists such as Francesco Lo Savio and Pino Pascali, whose work would lead into *Arte povera*.

Nature **(Natures)**

In the autumn of 1960, Fontana wrote to a friend about his recent *nature* sculptures, which were later cast in bronze (p. 111):

> I have worked a lot this summer at Albisola, I have made almost 30 balls in terracotta, very large, with large slashes and holes. I am very happy with them, it is nothingness! The death of material is the pure philosophy of life.[69]

It is evident from this account that Fontana regarded the irregular expressive openings within the dense terracotta as, in some sense, condensing negativity within the material. Just as the form of the cut relates closely to the contemporary *tagli* (p. 127), so does this ambition for dematerialisation. In another sense, the cavities in both series are openly sexual (scholars have alighted on *nature* as slang for female genitalia),[70] so that the sculptures conjoin physical and metaphysical connotations.

Nouveau Réalisme

In late 1960, the critic Pierre Restany encouraged a group of Parisian artists, who were already working in close collaboration, to form *Nouveau Réalisme*. The chosen name sought to indicate a new realism beyond that of literal transcription of the visible, but distinct from the isolation of abstraction. The artists included Arman, Yves Klein, Jean Tinguely and three artists who had been appropriating posters: Raymond Hains, Jacques Villeglé and François Dufrêne. The Roman artist Mimmo Rotella, who had been stripping posters from the streets of Rome since around 1952, joined the group in 1961. The group's purpose was as an alternative to the prevalence of *Informel*, and much of their initial output (from Klein's monochromes to Tinguely's drawing machines) reflected upon abstraction.

Of the French *Nouveaux Réalistes*, Klein was already well known in Italy because of his controversial solo exhibition *Proposte monocrome, epoca blu* (Monochrome propositions, blue period) held at the Galleria Apollinaire in January 1957. His eleven

Lucio Fontana
Natura, 1959–60, *Nature*
Bronze, 61 × 73 × 73 cm
Catalogo generale: 59-60 N 13 (see p. 135)
Tate, London

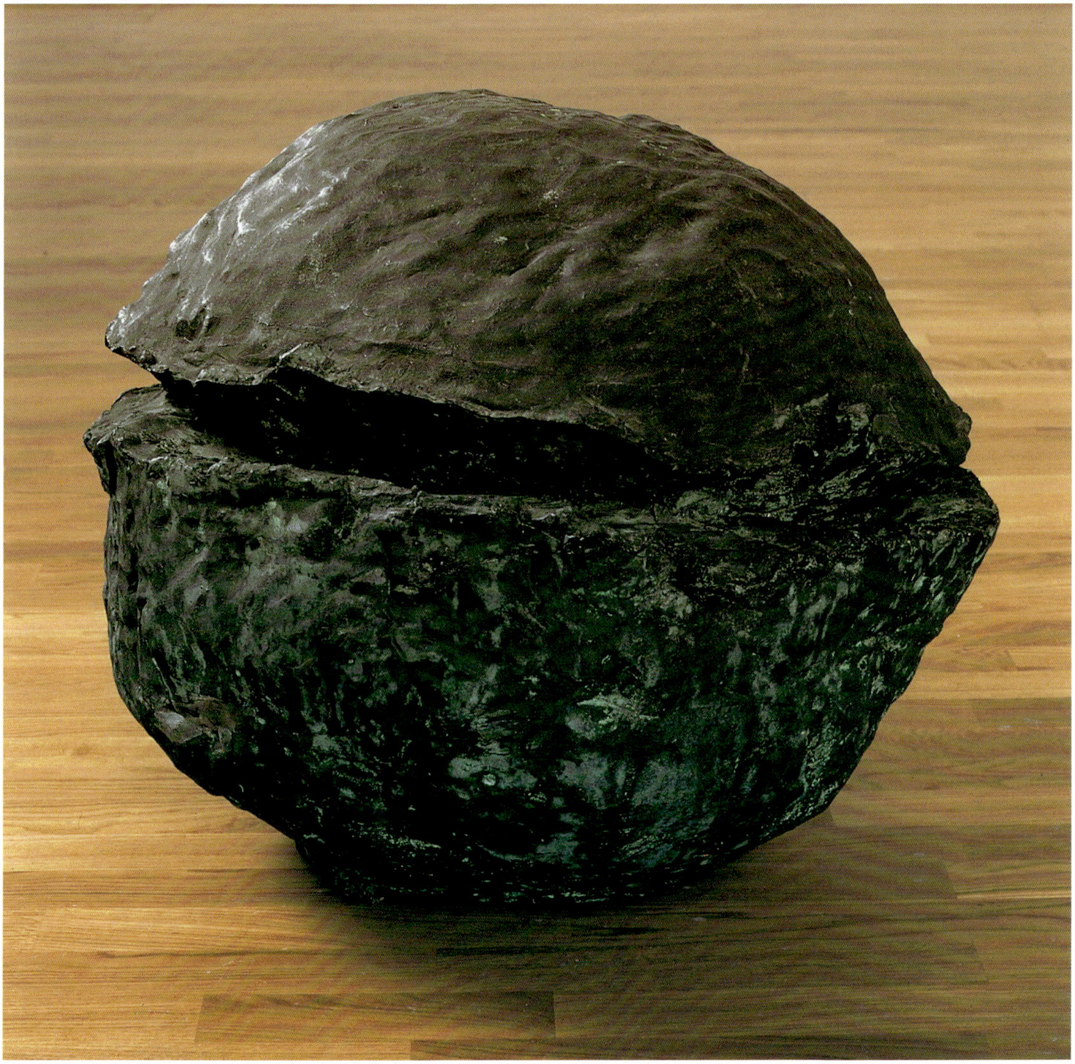

monochrome blue paintings caused a furore, partly because of their simplicity and partly because Restany's introduction to the exhibition catalogue compared them to Kasimir Malevich and to Giotto, writing of a 'phenomenon of pure *contemplation*'.[71] In common with Fontana, Klein eliminated the subject in favour of the gesture, although his gesture was to cover the surface with IKB (International Klein Blue) for maximum retinal saturation. Fontana so admired the result that he bought one of only three of the works that sold.[72] Manzoni was also a frequent visitor and met the artist there.[73] Klein's monochromes were a crucial impetus to his own *achromes*, even if, in place of colour, emotion and depth, Manzoni proposed neutrality.

Arte nucleare

Enrico Baj and Sergio Dangelo published the *Manifesto dell'arte nucleare* (Manifest of nuclear art) in February 1952. They posited, with ironic optimism, a new art for the nuclear age:

> Forms disintegrate: man's new forms are those of the atomic universe; the forms are electric charges. Ideal beauty … coincides with the representation of nuclear man and his space …
> Truth is not yours; it lies in the ATOM.
> Nuclear painting documents the search for this truth.[74]

Like *Spazialismo*, to which it was close in concept but distinguished by a thorough-going humanism, *Arte nucleare* upheld an idealistic view of scientific progress. It was established to generate artistic freedom and reject stylistic uniformity in favour of pictorial integrity. This was confirmed in the manifesto *Contro lo stile* (Against style) of September 1957 which marked a second, international, wave of activity; among the signatories were Fontana, Klein and Manzoni.

Nuvole (Clouds)

Among the later manifestations of Manzoni's *achromes* were the *nuvole*, fibreglass clouds, paradoxically captured in presentation boxes (p. 115). Their effect is somewhere between trapped beasts and the dislocated objects of René Magritte's paintings. With the contemporary polystyrene *achromes* (p. 121), the *nuvole* mark Manzoni's adoption of artificial materials.

Gruppo Origine

Burri was well connected in the Roman art world by the late 1940s and among his closest associates was the sculptor Ettore Colla. On Burri's failure to secure a travel bursary to Paris in

1948, it was apparently Colla who financed his trip.[75] Together with Giuseppe Capogrossi, one of the most significant painters working in Rome, and Mario Ballocco they founded the *Gruppo Origine* in January 1951. In retrospect, Burri recalled: 'I joined because they had asked me, because being part of a group could be useful. And then it did not seem fair to refuse.'[76] Although he also claimed not to have read the *Manifesto Origine* before its publication, it may be assumed that he broadly shared the group's views. The unsigned editorial in the first number of their periodical *Arti Visive* laid out their position:

> Every civilisation has left an image, whether in word or sign, the mark of its men and of its culture in history. In its cities, its streets, its spectacles, our civilisation offers a new visual world which is that of contemporary art, the language of which man no longer recognises even in its presence.
> As the forms of art and of thought unravel from the forms of life and of taste, so we want to redirect the contemporary to a language of art and redirect art to its profound and necessary reasons in human consciousness. To our work to create the images of our civilisation, we want to bring these writings whose purpose is exactly to educate modern man about the visual world of his days, about the consciousness of his nature at this time.[77]

Burri's work could certainly be located within this broad revisionist programme for a modern sensibility. His contribution to the *Origine* exhibition in 1953 was praised for its contemporaneity by the writer Emilio Villa: 'For each of these paintings we can always say: this is a work that can only have been done today, this is an action that could only have been performed today.'[78]

Panini (Bread rolls)

With the diversification of the *achromes* in 1960–1, Manzoni experimented with accumulations. These included the *panini* (p. 43), bread rolls whose regimentation (mimicking their arrangement for the oven) is reminiscent of the cotton-wool balls. Whereas the white of the cotton was integral, the rolls were coated in kaolin. While this must serve as a preservative, protecting the detail of the surface, it homogenised the colour and stripped away function. Like the eggs, also a staple food, that Manzoni adapted at the same time, the bread of the *panini* takes on a sacral aspect, the repetition alluding to daily experience.

Pietre (Stones)

A number of artists have mixed sand and stones with their paint

Piero Manzoni
Achrome, 1961–2
Fibreglass, 33 × 23.5 cm
Catalogo generale: 976 (see p. 135)
Archivio Piero Manzoni, Milan

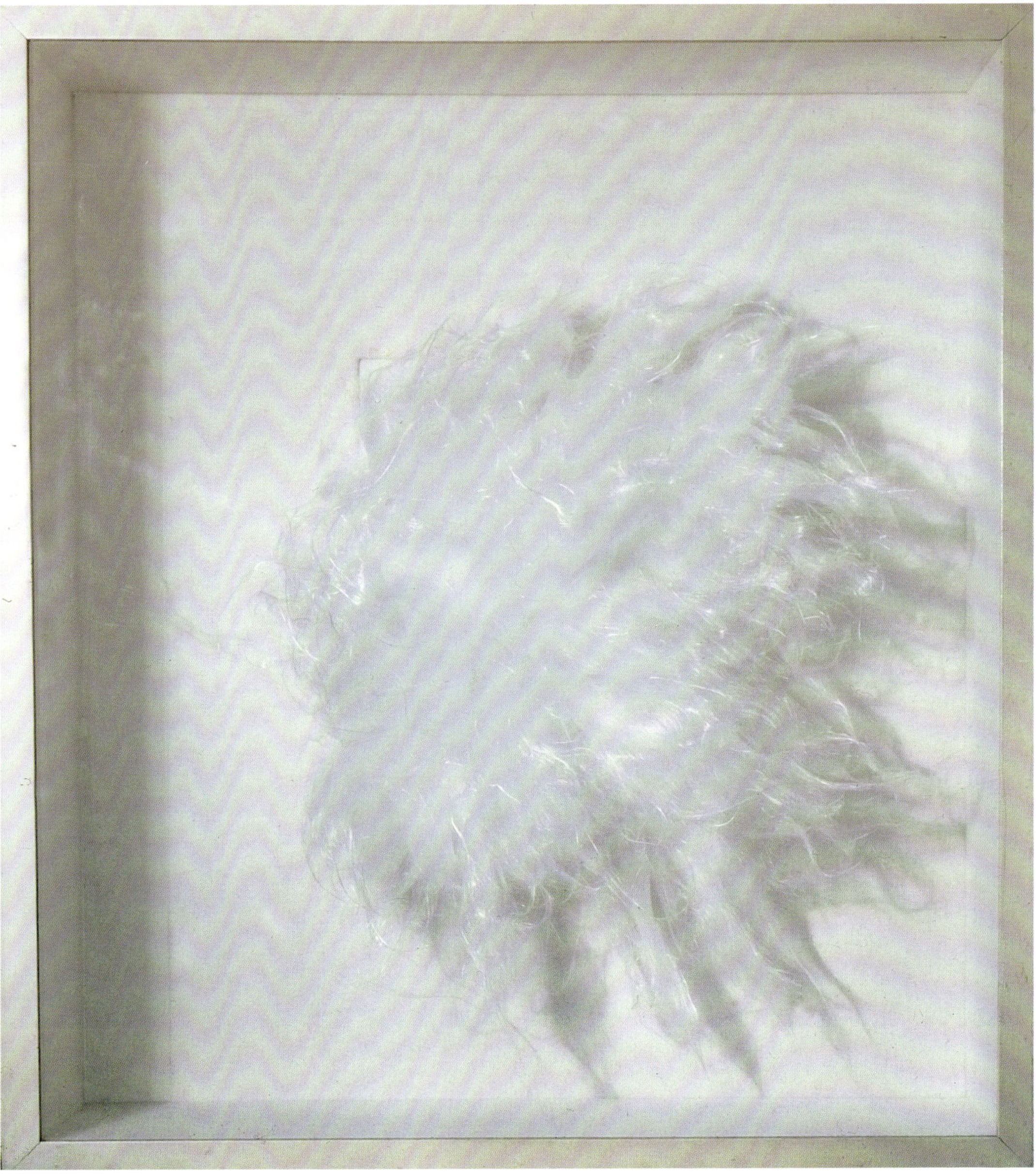

as a means of disrupting the picture surface. Burri used ground pumice stone in his early works (see p. 79), Fontana selected jewel-like *pietre* (which were actually glass) for certain *barocchi* and Manzoni embedded pebbles in his late achromes (p. 107). In each case the stones have augmented the density of the material impact of the work.

Plastic

In 1957 Roland Barthes identified plastic as 'the stuff of alchemy'. He went on:

> plastic is the very idea of its infinite transformation; as its everyday names indicates, it is ubiquity made visible. And it is this, in fact, which makes it a miraculous substance: a miracle is always a sudden transformation of nature. Plastic remains impregnated throughout with this wonder: it is less a thing than the trace of a movement ... But the price to be paid for this success is that plastic, sublimated as movement, hardly exists as substance.[79]

By the late 1950s, plastic had become a material as commonplace as those of nature (the constant counterpoint in Barthes's account), and was selected by artists for its very ubiquity. It was seen both as a miracle and a challenge.

In his *plastiche* Burri addressed many of the problems recognised by Barthes. While common – a symbol even of the economic health of Italy – plastic was tested to the extreme in the *combustioni* (pp. 53–4). What is different from the *legni*, in which fire was used to scorch and burn the surface, is that the material is transformed to the verge of destruction. With the flame, Burri worked at the edge of total loss, fashioning the warped and curdled material into a partially integrated residue (p. 119). He placed the plastic under unprecedented stress. Further, the process reveals the 'trace of a movement' in a way not anticipated by Barthes: the trace of the artist's controlled gesture. As such the power of the layered forms and delineated edges of the new material provided a contemporary extension of the *Informel*.

Maurizio Calvesi has remarked on the 'almost sadistic harshness of the wounds that Burri inflicted on his material',[80] and this violence is most acute in the works using fire: the *legni* and *plastiche*. While the technique parallels those of artists across Europe – notably Yves Klein, Jean Tinguely (in *Hommage to New York*, 1960) and, in Britain, Gustav Metzger with his *Auto-Destructive Art* – Burri attempted with the *plastiche* the very alchemical transformation of which Barthes wrote: to transform the unresponsive material of modern life into art. Whether he seeks beauty is difficult to determine. The rending of the membranous surface has a personalised sense of bodily violation that is powerful and terrifying, especially in the Cold War context.

It is telling to juxtapose Burri's stressed plastic with Manzoni's contemporary *polistiroli* (p. 121), *achromes* made from polystyrene (one of those substances that Barthes characterised as 'having names of Greek shepherds').[81] Like Burri, Manzoni transformed some by treating them with chemicals that attacked the surface. The majority, however, were presented unchanged for their inherent whiteness. Beyond a startling presentation as art of such an anonymous material (echoing Marcel Duchamp's readymades), they – together with the fibreglass *nuvole* (p. 115)– indicate an acceptance of the role of the artificial alongside Manzoni's, hitherto exclusively, natural materials. The remarkable aspect of this development is the inversion of expectations that this engenders. Through a typical paradox, the internal structure of the manmade polystyrene (like the fibreglass) is shown to be mesmerically chaotic, where Manzoni's ordering of the cotton grids (p. 87) establishes a uniformity and system in a natural substance (albeit in manufactured form).

Arte povera

In the fervid atmosphere of social unrest in 1967, the term *Arte povera* was coined by German Celant to identify the work of a cross-section of Italian artists working in conceptual ways and with unorthodox materials. He initially included Giovanni Anselmo, Piero Gilardi, Mario Merz, Gianni Piacentino, Michelangelo Pistoletto and Gilberto Zorio.[82] While the material experimentation and, to a lesser degree, the conceptual basis of *Arte povera* owed much to the generation of the 1950s – especially Burri, Fontana and Manzoni – the radicalised political position of the younger artists lent their work a completely different set of references. Burri, who was the only one among the three artists to live to see it, seems to have feared that his own achievement was somehow diminished by the success of the younger artists. Among those emerging in Rome who became key figures in *Arte povera* were Jannis Kounellis and Pino Pascali. Whatever Burri's anxieties, it is telling that Kounellis could recall the influences on Pascali thus:

> Pino loved American painting because he hated all of this chewed-up, putrefied culturalism in European painting (apart from Burri). In the beginning there is Pollock and Burri.[83]

Sacchi (Sacks)

Like Ettore Colla, his colleague in the *Gruppo Origine* in Rome, who reused the scrap-metal from wartime conflict for his

Alberto Burri
Rosso plastica,1962, *Red Plastic*
Plastic and combustion on canvas, 80 × 100 cm
Catalogo sistematico: 735 (see p. 135)
Fondazione Palazzo Albizzini 'Collezione Burri', Città di Castello

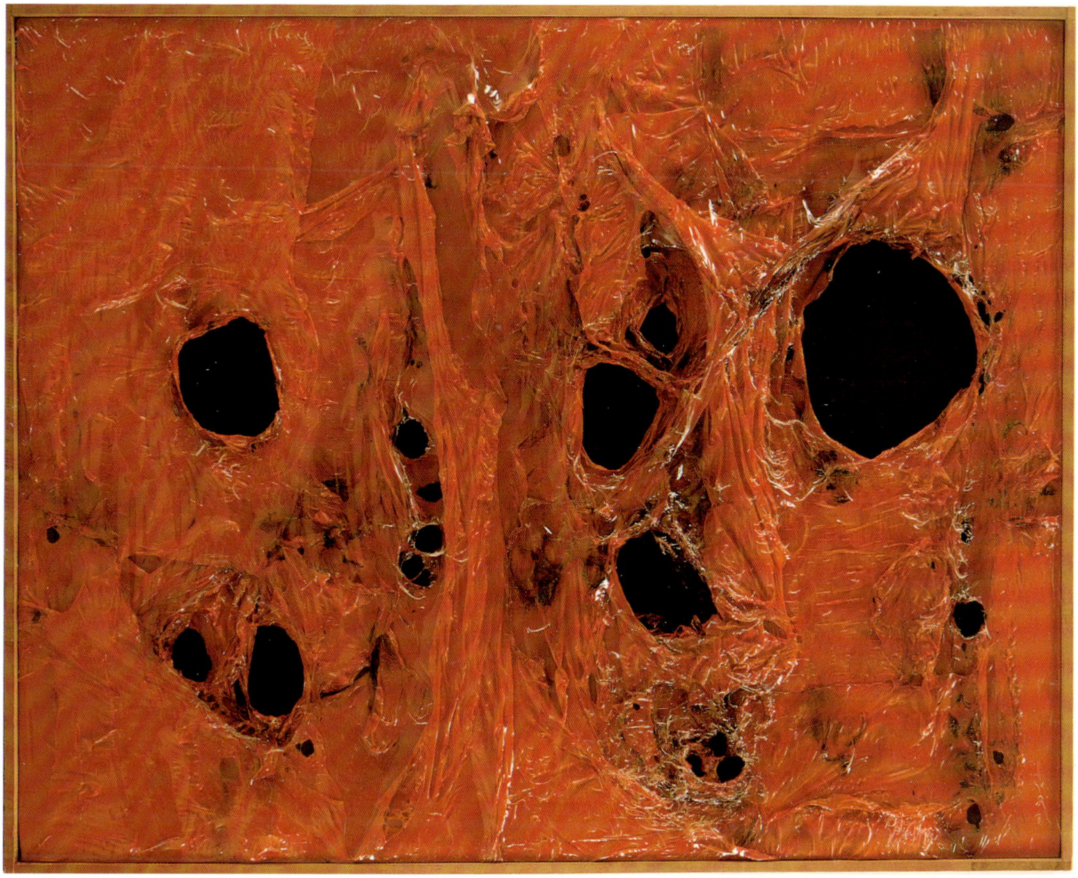

Piero Manzoni
Achrome, 1962–63
Polystyrene, 50 × 70 cm
Catalogo generale: 1123 (see p. 135)
Private collection

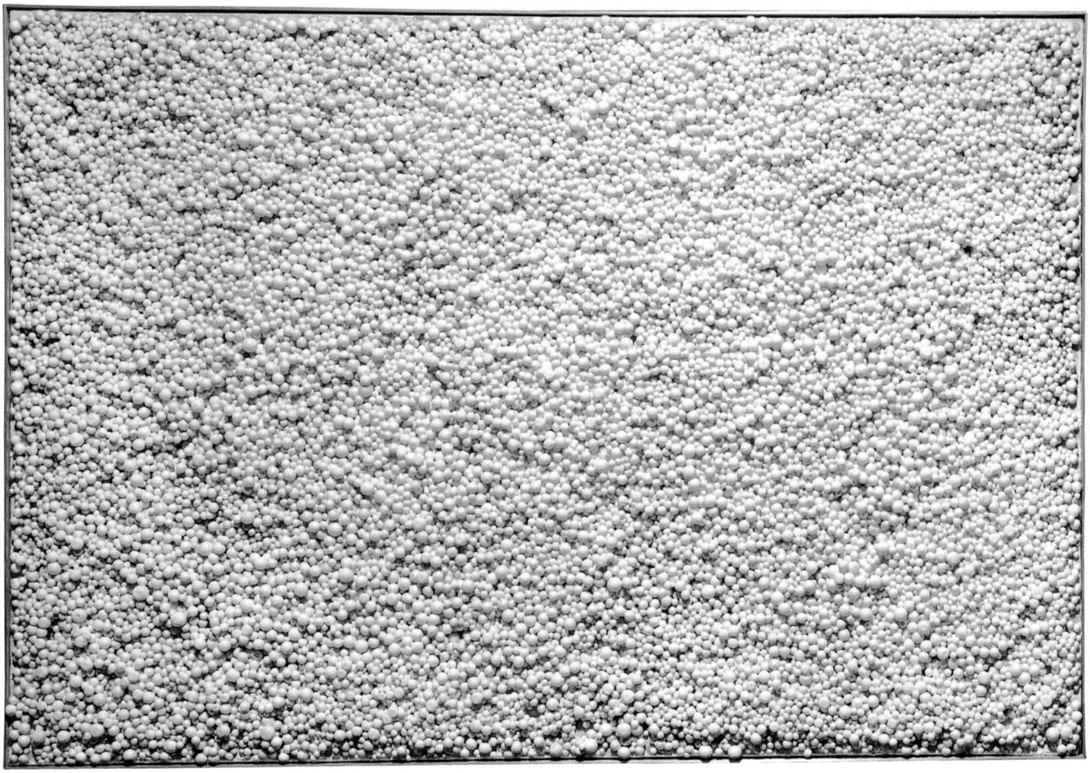

Alberto Burri
Sacco e oro, 1956, *Sacking and Gold*
Sacking, acrylic and gold on Cellotex, 52 × 44 cm
Catalogo sistematico: 276 (see p. 135)
Fondazione Palazzo Albizzini 'Collezione Burri', Città di Castello

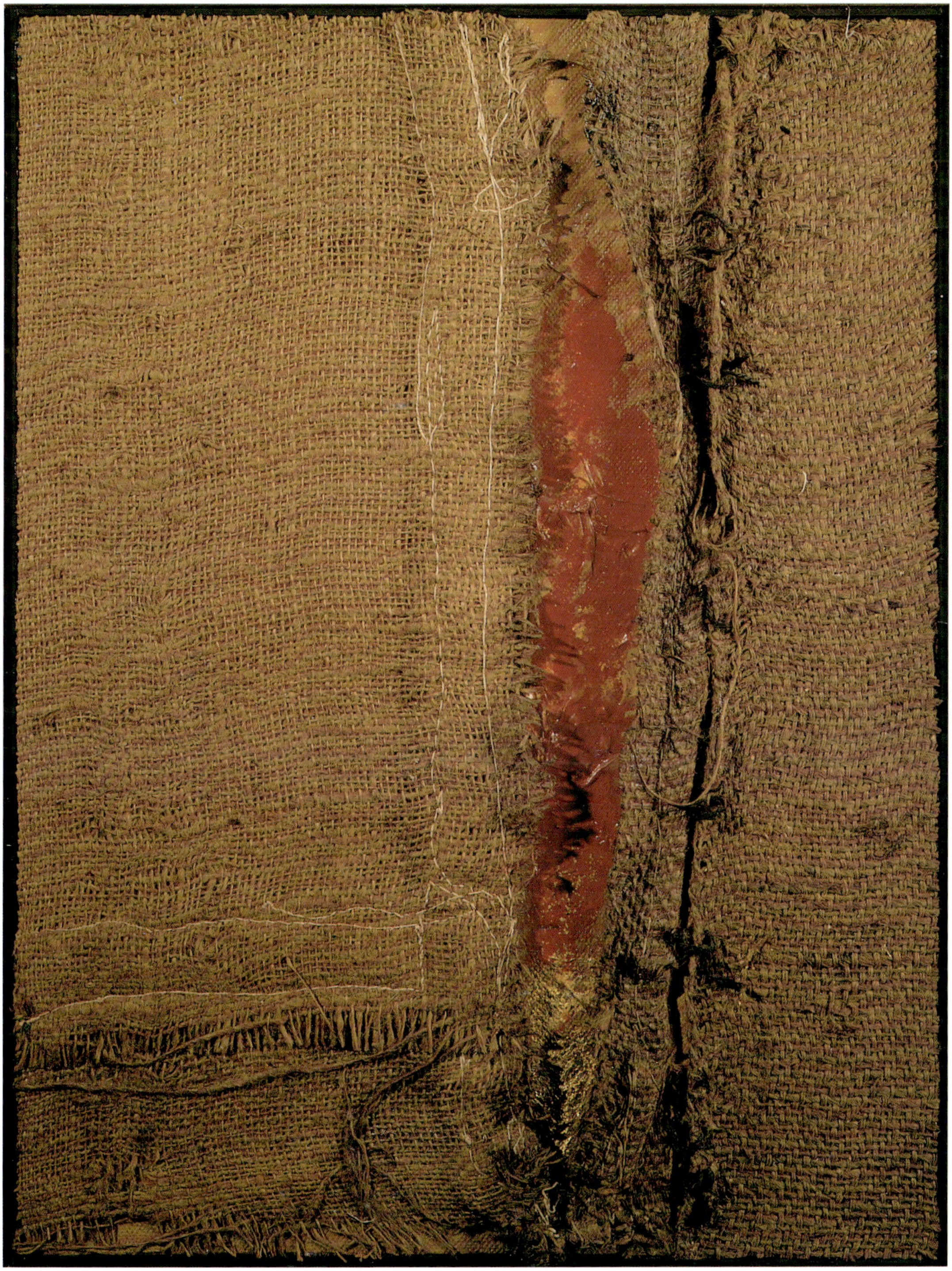

Lucio Fontana
Concetto spaziale 'Attesa', 1960, *Spatial Concept 'Waiting'*
Canvas, 93 × 73 cm
Catalogo generale: 60 T 13 (see p. 135)
Tate, London

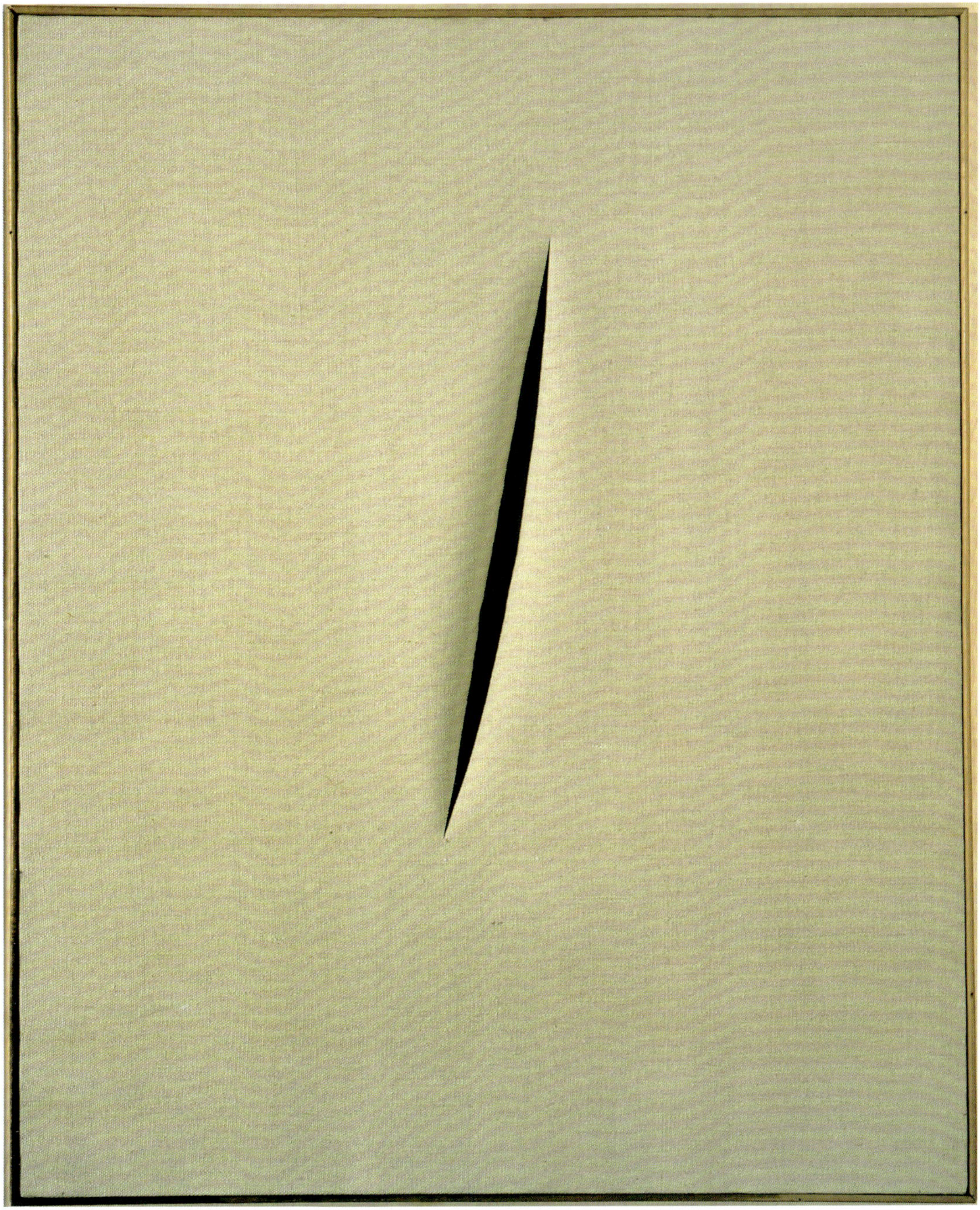

Tagli (Cuts)

Writing of the *tagli*, Fontana's canvases with single or multiple cuts (p. 127), begun in 1959, Enrico Crispolti remarked on their achievement in the 'opening up of an entirely new vision of absolute, almost metaphysical, character'.[91] The gesture returned Fontana to the simple physicality of the earlier *buchi*, though it is immediately apparent that this is achieved by contrasting means. The cuts are a trace of a ritualised process. 'I really have to be in the right mood to perform this task' he told the photographer Ugo Mulas and the photographs that resulted were, in fact, a re-enactment for the camera.[92] Fontana's procedure was to cut into the painted canvas when it was still damp. When fully dry he opened the cut 'using the hand as a blade', as Sarah Whitfield has revealed, 'a gesture described by a close friend of Fontana's who witnessed it as a "caress"'.[93] The opening thus created was held in place and backed with black cloth so as to achieve an evocation of infinity. Interestingly the (anonymous) friend's choice of the word 'caress' to describe the action also evokes a sexuality that is latent in these works.

Venice Biennale

The post-war revival of the Venice Biennale in 1948 was a significant event in the art world. The tiers of selection committees, invitations and prizes were complex, and the decisions were regularly controversial. Even the award to Giorgio Morandi of the *Comune di Venezia* prize at the 1948, in the year of the dominance of the Communist paintings of Renato Guttuso and the artists of the *Fronte Nuovo delle arti* (New front of the arts), provoked debate. In retrospect, the 1948 Biennale has been seen as significant for the display of Peggy Guggenheim's collection of Surrealist and recent American art, though it is notable that such a well-informed witness as the painter Piero Dorazio recalled that it was 'presented in disorder, without historic or critical information and without any real interest to a crowd of pagans'.[94] It was certainly significant as a debut for Abstract Expressionism and specifically for Jackson Pollock, whose work Guggenheim showed at the Museo Correr in 1950. When Lionello Venturi presented the gestural abstraction of the *Gruppo degli Otto* at the 1952 Biennale, Pollock's pervasive influence (whether actual or not) seemed to be confirmed.

The Biennale saw controversy around both Burri and Fontana. In 1952, the selection committee rejected two of Burri's *sacchi,* though they did accept two works that presented the same composition in more orthodox ways. At the following Biennale, in 1954, Fontana provoked only notoriety and incomprehension by showing nine *buchi*. Nevertheless, it would lead to the major solo room in 1958, which generated admiration even from critics such as Venturi, who confessed to have 'insufficient fantasy to follow him'.[95] For his part, Burri showed three important works that year (introduced by James Johnson Sweeney, Director of the Guggenheim) and went on to win the AICI prize at the 1960 Biennale.

This period saw the confirmation of *Informel* in Venice. Prizes were awarded to Afro Basaldella (1956), Mark Tobey (the International Prize in 1958), Franz Kline (1960) and Giuseppe Capogrossi (1962). This made the award of the Grand Prize in 1964 to Robert Rauschenberg an acute break: just as Pollock's arrival has been understood as the triumph of American Abstract Expressionism, so Rauschenberg's recognition seemed like the triumph of American Pop.

The Void

Many works of the period seem to relate to the void, whether masking or providing a glimpse into it. Fontana confronted it with apparent optimism: 'I am seeking to represent the void. Humanity, accepting the idea of Infinity, has already accepted the idea of Nothingness. And today Nothingness is a mathematical formula.'[96] *Spazialismo* thus provided a means to explore the dynamism of man's creativity. In cutting the illusory surface of the canvas, Fontana opened it onto an intangible potential beyond. Although it is evident in some of Fontana's works – especially the *nature* – Burri's practice entailed an ordering of the world through touch as much as vision. The tactile surface is thrust forward at the viewer, demanding attention for its complexity. This tactility makes the frequent holes all the more immeasurable as apparent degradation plays to a general anxiety of disintegration.

Zero

During 1957, the Düsseldorf-based artists Heinz Mack, Otto Piene and Günther Uecker held 'evening exhibitions', which specifically rejected the commercial structure of the art world. Their work was concerned with light rather than form, and they were inspired by Yves Klein's monochromes (seen at his exhibition in Düsseldorf in May 1957). At the seventh evening exhibition, *Das Rote Bild* (The red picture), in April 1958 they launched their periodical *Zero*. The name signified a radical simplification of art which chimed with many across Europe, not least the artists of *Arte nucleare*. Their reduction of form – seen in Uecker's nail pictures and Piene's use of smoke – was based in what Piene called a 'new idealism' (as distinct from *Nouveau Réalisme*). They sought a public aspect for art and this combined with their

[30] Burri, 'Statement', in Andrew C. Ritchie (ed.), *The New Decade*, exh. cat., Museum of Modern Art, New York 1955, p. 82.

[31] Milton Gendel, 'Burri Makes a Picture', *Art News*, vol. 3, 1954, pp. 28–30, 67.

[32] James Johnson Sweeney, *Burri*, L'Obelisco, Rome 1955, p. 5.

[33] Giuliano Serafini, *Burri: La misura e il fenomeno / The Measure and the Phenomenon*, Charta, Milan 1999, p. 181.

[34] See Italo Calvino, *Marcovaldo*, Einaudi, Turin 1963, trans. William Weaver, Martin Secker & Warburg, London 1983.

[35] Maurizio Calvesi, *Burri inedito; Seen / Unseen Burri*, exh. cat., Ex Seccatoi del Tabacco, Città di Castello 2000, p. 21.

[36] Rosenberg 1962, p. 25.

[37] Maurizio Fagiolo dell'Arco, *L'Arte oggi in Italia: Rapporto 60*, Bulzoni, Rome 1966, p. 70, cited in Serafini 1999, p. 176.

[38] Gaston Bachelard, *La Psychoanalyse du feu*, Paris 1938, as *The Psychoanalysis of Fire*, trans. Alan M. Ross, Beacon Press, Boston 1964, p. 7, cited in Sidra Stich, *Yves Klein*, exh. cat., Hayward Gallery, London 1995, p. 227.

[39] Fontana, letter to Charles Damiano, Feb. 1959, quoted in Alloway 1959, p. 5.

[40] Fontana, interview with Daniela Palazzoli, *Bit*, no. 5, Oct.-Nov. 1967, cited in Whitfield 1999, p. 136.

[41] Carlo Carrà, *L'attesa*, 1926 and Arturo Martini, *L'attesa* or *La veglia*, 1930–1, both in private collections.

[42] Manzoni, 'Some Realisations, Some Experiments, Some Projects', trans. in *Piero Manzoni: Painting, Reliefs & Objects* 1974, p. 84.

[43] Ibid., p. 85.

[44] Martina Cardelli, 'Entretien avec Ettore Sordini', in Martina Cardelli and Danielle Rhan (eds.), *Piero Manzoni, Contre rien*, Editions Allia, Paris 2002, p. 60; my translation from French (translated from the original Italian).

[45] Jean-Paul Sartre, *La Nausée*, Gallimard, Paris 1938; first trans. 1949, and as *Nausea*, trans. Robert Baldick, Penguin Books, Harmondsworth 1965. Albert Camus, *L'Etranger*, Paris 1940, as *The Outsider*, trans. Stuart Gilbert, Hamish Hamilton, London 1946 and Penguin Books, Harmondsworth 1965.

[46] Serafini 1999, p. 121.

[47] Maurice Merleau-Ponty, *La Phénoménologie de la perception*, Gallimard, Paris 1945; trans. as *The Phenomenology of Perception*, Routledge, London 1962; cited in Thomas Baldwin (ed.), *Maurice Merleau-Ponty: Basic Writings*, Routledge, London and New York 2004, p. 75.

[48] Maurice Merleau-Ponty, *L'Œil et l'esprit*, Gallimard, Paris 1964; trans. as *Eye and Mind*, Northwestern University Press, Evanston 1964; cited in Baldwin 2004, pp. 318–19.

[49] Calvesi 2000, p. 21.

[50] Unsourced quotation in Serafini 1999, p. 181.

[51] Fontana et al., *Manifiesto blanco*, Buenos Aires 1946, trans. in Ades 1989, pp. 331–4.

[52] See Fontana, letters to Pablo Edelstein, 1949–51, in Campiglio 1999, pp. 105–25

[53] See Renato Miracco's essay above.

[54] Fontana, letter to Pablo Edelstein, 4 Feb. 1952, ibid., letter 117, p. 126; my translation.

[55] Ballo, 1959, [p. 2].

[56] Yve-Alain Bois, 'The Use Value of "Formless"', in Yve-Alain Bois and Rosalind E. Krauss, *Formless: A User's Guide*, Zone Books, New York 1997, p. 28.

[57] Fontana, letter to Gio Ponti, 30 July 1951, in Campiglio 1999, letter 261, p. 219; my translation.

[58] Milton Gendel, 'Burri Makes a Picture', *Art News*, vol. 3, 1954, pp. 28–30, 67.

[59] Hannah Arendt, 'Introduction: Walter Benjamin: 1892–1940', in Walter Benjamin, *Illuminations*, trans. Harry Zohn, Jonathan Cape, London 1970 and Fontana, London 1973, pp. 1–10.

[60] Manzoni, 'Some Realisations, Some Experiments, Some Projects', trans. in *Piero Manzoni: Painting, Reliefs & Objects*, 1974, p. 84.

[61] Jen Jørgen Thorsen, 'Han saelger ideer på dåser', *Aktuelt* (Copenhagen), 20 June 1960, republished in Italian in Giorgio

Zanchetti, 'Progetti immediate di llibertà integrale. Percorsi dell'uovo e dell'impronta intorno a Piero Manzoni', in Negri 2002, Appendix 2, p. 231.

[62] Michio Hayashi, 'The Occupied Subject: Painting and Body in Post-war Japan', in Dore Ashton (ed.), *A Rebours: La Rebelión Informalista / The Informal Rebellion*, exh. cat., Museo Nacional Centro de Arte Reina Sofía, Madrid 1999, pp. 61–2.

[63] Maurizio Calvesi, '*Informel* and Abstraction in Italian Art of the Fifties', in Emily Braun (ed.), *Italian Art of the 20th Century*, exh. cat., Royal Academy, London 1989, p. 289.

[64] See Serafini 1999, p. 176 citing Werner Haftmann, *Enciclopedia della pittura moderna*, Il Saggiatore, Milan 1960, p. 500, trans. as *Painting in the Twentieth Century*, Lund Humphries, London 1960, p. 362.

[65] Manzoni, 1960, p. 19.

[66] Burri, 1955, p. 82.

[67] Manzoni, letter to Valentino Dori, undated [?March 1958], in Freddy Battino and Luca Palazzoli, *Piero Manzoni: Catalogue raisonné*, Vanni Scheiwiller, Milan 1991, p. 31.

[68] Manzoni, 'Libera dimensione', 1960, p. 19.

[69] Fontana, letter to Jef Verheyen, 5 October 1960, in Campiglio 1999, letter 197, pp. 179–80; my translation.

[70] Marianne Brouwer cited in Yve-Alain Bois, 'Fontana's Base Materialism', *Art in America*, vol. 77, April 1989, p. 279.

[71] Cited in Sidra Stich, *Yves Klein*, exh. cat., Hayward Gallery, London 1995, p. 81.

[72] Ibid. p. 82.

[73] Anna Costantini, 'Piero Manzoni in Context 1933–1963', in Celant 1998, p. 261.

[74] Reprinted in *Arte Nucleare, 1951–1957*, Galleria San Fedele, Milan 1980, p. 37; trans. in Stich 1995, p. 260.

[75] Serafini 1999, pp. 17, 128.

[76] Ibid., p. 153.

[77] Unsigned editorial, *Arti Visive: Rivista della Fondazione Origine*, July–August 1952, front [p. 1]; my translation.

[78] Emilio Villa, cited in Serafini 1999, p. 141.

[79] Roland Barthes, 'Plastic', in *Mythologies*, Editions du Seuil, Paris 1957, selected and trans. by Annette Lavers, Granada Publishing, London 1973, p. 97.

[80] Maurizio Calvesi, in Braun 1989, p. 290.

[81] Barthes 1973, p. 97.

[82] Richard Flood and Frances Morris, 'Introduction', in Richard Flood and Frances Morris (eds.), *Zero to Infinity: Arte Povera 1962–1972*, exh. cat., Tate Modern, London, and Walker Art Center, Minneapolis 2001, p. 10.

[83] Jannis Kounellis, statement on Pino Pascali, *Qui Arte Contemporanea*, no. 5, March 1969, p. 23, trans. ibid., p. 287.

[84] Giuliano Briganti, 'Cultural Provocation: Italian Art of the Early Sixties', in Braun 1989, p. 303.

[85] Fabrizio D'Amico (ed.), *Roma 1950–59: Il rinnovamento della pittura in Italia*, Ferrara 1996, p. 138, cited in Serafini 1999, p. 160.

[86] See Celant 1993, pp. 19–23.

[87] Bois 1997, p. 31.

[88] Fontana, draft letter to Giampiero Giani, 2 Nov. 1949, in Campiglio 1999, p. 243; my translation.

[89] Quoted in Whitfield 1999, p. 185.

[90] Fontana, 'Technical Manifesto Given at the 1st International Congress of Proportion at the IXth Triennale Milan, 1947' [sic], trans. Charles Damiano, *Ark, Journal of the Royal College of Art*, Winter 1959, no. 24, p. 7.

[91] In Van der Mack and Crispolti 1974, p. 136; translation slightly modified from that published.

[92] Ugo Mulas, *La fotografia*, Turin 1973, p. 100, cited in Jole de Sanna 1993, pp. 120–1.

[93] Whitfield 1999, p. 31.

[94] Piero Dorazio, '*La 26° Biennale di Venezia*: ancora il realismo', *Arti Visive: Rivista della Fondazione Origine*, July–Aug. 1952, p. 7; my translation.

[95] Lionello Venturi, 'Biennale di Venezia', *L'Espresso*, 22 June 1958, cited in Zanchetti 2002, p. 194; my translation.

[96] Fontana, interview with Nerio Mi-

Chronology

ALBERTO BURRI

Born 12 March 1915, Città di Castello, Umbria, son of a wine merchant.
Interrupts medical studies (1934–40) to volunteer for Abyssinian war (1935). Called up (1941) and captured (1943) while serving as military doctor in North Africa. Sent as prisoner-of-war to Hereford, Texas; begins to paint. Returns to Italy (1946), settling in Rome.

LUCIO FONTANA

Born 19 February 1899, Rosario de Santa Fé, Argentina, son of a commercial sculptor from Varese, Italy. The family moves to Italy in 1905. Fights in First World War (aged seventeen). Five years (1922–7) with family firm in Argentina, before studying sculpture under Adolfo Wildt at Brera in Milan. In 1930s shows at Galleria Il Milione and joins Paris-based *Abstraction-Création* (1935). Leaves for Argentina in 1940; appointed Professor at Escuela Nacional, Buenos Aires (1945) and (1946) co-founds Altamira school where *Manifiesto blanco* is published by his students. Father dies.

PIERO MANZONI

Born 13 July 1933, Soncino near Cremona; son of Conte Egisto di Chiosca e Poggiolo, a businessman in the food industry. Brought up in Milan and Soncino with summers in Soprazocco (Lake Garda) and Albisola.

1946

Fourth Republic established in France.
Nuremberg trials.
Abdication of Vittorio Emanuele III and declaration of Italian Republic (June) with Alcide de Gasperi as acting head of state.

1947

Burri: First solo show (figurative works) at Galleria La Margherita, Rome (July).

***Forma 1* (Rome) promotes abstract art while *Fronte nuovo delle arti* (Milan) defends post-Cubism.**

Fontana: Returns to Milan (April). With Beniamino Joppolo, Giorgio Kaisserlian and Milena Milani publishes *Primo manifesto dello spazialismo* (Dec.).

De Gasperi expels Communists and Socialists from Italian government.
Marshall Plan endorsed in Switzerland.

1948

Burri: Knows Enrico Prampolini and Art Club circle. Visits Paris and sees Jean Dubuffet's works. Shows *catrami* (tars) at Galleria La Margherita, Rome, and Galleria dell'Angelo, Città di Castello.

Venice: Biennale prize-winners include Giorgio Morandi and Henry Moore. Peggy Guggenheim's exhibition includes Arshile Gorky, Jackson Pollock, and Robert Motherwell.

Fontana: *Secondo manifesto dello spazialismo* co-signed with Joppolo, Kaisserlian, Milani, Giani Dova and Antonino Tullier (March); shows sculptures at Venice Biennale.

Harry S. Truman wins US Presidential election.

ALBERTO BURRI	LUCIO FONTANA	PIERO MANZONI	
Paints *SZ1*, on sack with US flag, and *bianchi* (whites). Included in Art Club exhibition at Galleria Nazionale d'Arte Moderna, Rome, and in *Salon des Réalistes Nouvelles*, Paris.	Makes *Ambiente spaziale a luce nera* (Spatial environment with black light) with phosphorescent paint at Galleria del Naviglio. Included in *Twentieth Century Italian Art* at the Museum of Modern Art (New York). Begins *buchi* series.	Mao Tse-Tung forms Communist Republic in China. Federal Republic of Germany declared with Konrad Adenauer as Chancellor. Berlin blockade by East Germany broken by air-lift.	1949
Aged thirty-five. Begins to make *muffe*, *gobbi* and *sacchi* (moulds, hunchbacks and sacks). Rome: First solo shows of Carla Accardi (Age d'Or) and Giuseppe Capogrossi (Galleria del Secolo). Venice: Realist Biennale includes Guttuso; Pollock show at Museo Correr.	Aged fifty-one. Exhibits ceramics at Galleria Il Milione. Unimpressed by Picasso's ceramics at Vallauris. Enters competition for doors of Duomo in Milan.	Aged seventeen. While still at school begins to paint, making figurative works.	1950
With Mario Ballocco, Giuseppe Capogrossi and Ettore Colla co-founds *Gruppo Origine*. Shows a *gobbo* in *Arte astratta e concreta in Italia* at Galleria Nazionale d'Arte Moderna.	Makes neon *Ambiente* at Milan Triennale; reads *Manifesto tecnico dello spazialismo* there (May). Contributes to 1st São Paulo *Bienal*, Brazil. Signs fourth *Manifesto* (Nov.). Uses coloured glass for *pietre* (stones).	Studies Law at Università Cattolica del Sacro Cuore, Milan (until December 1954).	1951
Neri e muffe (Blacks and moulds) show at Galleria dell'Obelisco (Jan.); *13 Opere di Burri* at Galleria d'Arte Contemporanea, Florence. Moves to Via Margutta; Robert Rauschenberg and Cy Twombly see his work. *Sacchi* rejected by Art Club and by Venice Biennale. Signs *Manifesto del movimento spaziale per la televisione*.	Shows *buchi* in *Arte spaziale*, Galleria del Naviglio, Milan (Feb.); followed by solo show there in May–June. Publishes *Manifesto del movimento spaziale per la televisione* (May), also signed by Crippa, Dova, Tancredi and, among others, Burri; makes experimental television broadcast. Marries Teresita Rasini and moves studio to Corso Monforte.	H-Bomb tested by US at Eniwetok Atoll in Pacific. General Eisenhower elected US President. Brussels: Enrico Baj and Sergio Dangelo write *Manifesto dell'arte nucleare*. Venice: Biennale includes Afro and *Gruppo degli Otto*. Alexander Calder wins Sculpture prize.	1952
Solo show at Fondazione Origine (April). James Johnson Sweeney (new Director of Solomon R. Guggenheim Museum, New York) secures first US show: *Alberto Burri: Paintings and Collages* at Allan	Solo show of *buchi* at Galleria del Naviglio. *Fiore* (flower) sculptures prove controversial in *Biennale de la Sculpture* at Middleheim Park, Antwerp. Agnoldomenico Pica publishes: *Fontana e lo spazialismo*.	New York: Twombly and Rauschenberg show precedes Burri's at Stable Gallery. Rome: Picasso retrospective at Galleria Nazionale d'Arte Moderna and Palazzo Reale, Milan.	1953

	ALBERTO BURRI	LUCIO FONTANA	PIERO MANZONI
	Frumkin Gallery, Chicago (April) and Stable Gallery, New York (Nov.). Sweeney includes Burri and Capogrossi in *Younger European Painters: A Selection* at the Guggenheim.		**Coronation of Elizabeth II. Italian Government formed by Giuseppe Pella. Death of Stalin; political thaw under Nikita Khrushchev. Tito elected Yugoslav President.**
1954	Solo show at Galleria dell'Obelisco, Milan (April); critic Milton Gendel publishes 'Burri Makes a Picture' (*Art News*). Second Chicago show at Frumkin, and included in group show at Martha Jackson Gallery, New York. Begins *combustioni* on paper.	Shows 10 sculptures and 9 *buchi* at Venice Biennale. Serves on the committee of Milan *Triennale* and participates in *Incontro internazionale di ceramisti* at Albisola. Begins chalk-pastel *gessi* (plasters), and *barocchi*.	While still studying Law, frequents Milanese art scene, including Galleria Schwarz exhibitions of Duchamp and of Schwitters. **Venice: Biennale prize-winners include Max Ernst, Jean Arp and Joan Miró. Willem De Kooning shows in US pavilion; Francis Bacon and Lucian Freud in British pavilion.**
1955	Marries American dancer Minsa Craig. Travels to New York for inclusion in *New Decade: 22 European Painters and Sculptors* (Museum of Modern Art) and solo show (Stable Gallery); also has *Collages of Alberto Burri* touring from Fine Arts Center, Colorado Springs. Sweeney publishes first monograph and introduces show at Milan Triennale. Included in 3rd São Paulo *Bienal*, and Carnegie Institute's Pittsburgh International.	Solo show of *pietre* at Galleria del Naviglio (Feb.) and, in March, of ceramics at Galleria dello Zodiaco, Rome. In summer participates in *Il Gesto: rassegna internazionale delle forme libere*, Galleria Schettini, Milan.	Changes course and university, enrolling (Jan.) in second year Philosophy course at University of Rome. Spends about a year in Rome. **Albisola: Asger Jorn and others propose experimental *Bauhaus immaginista*. Milan: *Movimento nucleare* launches periodical *Il Gesto*. Death of Albert Einstein.**
1956	Begins *Combustioni legni*. Show at Galleria del Cavallino, Venice and included in Biennale. Shares two-person show with César at Galerie Rive Droite, Paris. Shows in *Italienische Malerei Heute*, Stadtisches Museum Leverkusen. **Suez Crisis, Egyptian nationalisation of Canal followed by repulsion of French and British invasion. Hungarian uprising crushed by USSR and Warsaw Pact.**	Exhibition at Galleria del Naviglio marks decade of *Spazialismo* (May–June) and Giampiero Giani publishes *Spazialismo: origine e sviluppi di una tendenza artistica*. Included in *Italian Art of the 20th Century* exhibition touring Australia. **New York: Pollock dies in car crash (Aug.). Venice: Afro wins Comune di Venezia prize at Biennale; Franz Kline represents USA.**	Transfers to Philosophy course at University of Milan but abandons studies. Shows hominoids at *Mostra mercato* in Soncino (Aug.) and makes works with tar and imprints. Publishes *Per la scoperta di una zona d'immagini* with Camillo Corvi-Mora, Ettore Sordini and Giuseppe Zecca (Dec.).

Year	ALBERTO BURRI	LUCIO FONTANA	PIERO MANZONI
1957	First Milan solo show (Galleria del Naviglio) overlaps with Klein show (Galleria Apollinaire, Jan.). Shows with Afro and Toti Scialoja (La Tartaruga, Rome). Premiers *combustioni* at Galleria dell'Obelisco (May). *Paintings by Alberto Burri*, organised by Sweeney for Carnegie Institute, Pittsburgh in November. **Rome: Dorazio and Colla shows at Galleria La Tartaruga. Frances McCann establishes Rome-New York Foundation. Twombly settles in Rome.**	Two solo shows at Galleria del Naviglio, Milan (Feb. and Nov.). Included in *Arte italiana dal 1910 a oggi*, Haus der Kunst, Munich, and *Between Space and Earth: Trends in Modern Italian Art*, Marlborough Fine Art, London. Makes installation for Milan *Triennale* using coloured glass. Completes *barocchi* series. **NATO locates thermo-nuclear warheads at Italian bases. European Economic Community established with Treaty of Rome.**	Impressed by Klein and Burri shows in January. With Sordini and Angelo Verga, publishes *L'arte non è vera creazione* (Art is not true creation) for three-man show at Galleria Pater (May); catalogue introduced by Fontana. Joins *Arte nucleare*. With others signs *Manifesto di Albisola Marina* (Aug.) and *Contro lo stile* (Against style). Contributes to *Arte nucleare* show (Galleria San Fedele, November). Begins to make *achromes* with kaolin.
1958	*Paintings by Alberto Burri* tours to Chicago, Buffalo and San Francisco. Show at Galleria La Salita, Rome (March). Begins *ferri* which he shows at Galleria Blu, Milan (Nov.). Has three works in Venice Biennale. **Rome: Pollock retrospective at Galleria Nazionale d'Arte Moderna. Venice: Biennale includes Wols retrospective, works by Johns and Rothko; Mark Tobey wins Grand Prize.**	Exhibits with Manzoni and Baj in Bergamo; 27 works at Venice Biennale introduced by Guido Ballo. Signs *VII Manifesto tecnico dello spazialismo*. Included in *International Art of a New Era: Informel & Gutaï*, Osaka, and *Pittura italiana contemporanea*, Galleria Nazionale d'Arte Moderna, Rome. **Milan: *The New American Painting* showing Abstract Expressionists at Civica Galleria d'Arte Moderna.**	Three-person show with Baj and Fontana (Galleria Bergamo, Bergamo, Jan.), followed by second Galleria Pater show (April–May). Included in *L'avanguardia* (Galleria Montenapoleone, May) with Picabia, Sant'Elia, Fontana and Baj. Visits Netherlands and Paris. With Baj and Sergio Dangelo co-edits *Il Gesto 3* (Sept.). **Düsseldorf: Heinz Mack, Otto Piene and Günther Uecker form *Zero*; *Dada* exhibition at Städtische Kunsthalle.**
1959	Two shows in Basel: at Galerie Marie-Suzanne Feigel (Feb.–March) and Galerie Beyeler, shared with Tapies (May–June). Solo shows in May at Galleria La Tartaruga, Rome, and Galleria Loggia, Bologna. Exhibition, introduced by Giulio Carlo Argan, at Palais des Beaux-Arts in Brussels (April). Included in 5th São Paulo *Bienal* and *Documenta II*, Kassel.	Begins *tagli* and first shows them in *Painting from the Damiano Collection*, Institute of Contemporary Arts, London, then in Milan (Naviglio) and Paris (Galerie Städler). Contributes to *5th Sculpture Biennale* at Middleheimpark in Antwerp, *Documenta II*, and 5th São Paulo *Bienal*. Makes and shows *nature* in Albisola. Crispolti organises retrospective at Galleria l'Attico, Rome and Galleria Notizie, Turin (Oct.–Nov.). Gillo Dorfles publishes monograph.	Departure from *Nucleare* marked by *Bonalumi, Castellani, Manzoni* shows in Milan (Galleria del Prisma, Feb.) Rome (Galleria Appia Antica) and Lausanne (Galerie Kasper). In *Zero* group shows at Rotterdamsche Kunstring and Galerie Boukes, Wiesbaden. Begins *lines*. With Castellani publishes *Azimuth* and opens Azimut gallery (Dec.). **Rome: Accardi, Rotella, Scarpitta and others in *Giovane pittura di Roma*, Galleria La Tartaruga. Mario Schifano's first show at Galleria Appia Antica. De Kooning working in Rome.**

	ALBERTO BURRI	LUCIO FONTANA	PIERO MANZONI
1960	Moves to Grottarossa outside Rome. Holds solo show at Martha Jackson Gallery, New York (Feb.) and Hanover Gallery, London (March–April). Room at Venice Biennale wins AICI prize. Included in *Burri, Consagra, De Kooning, Matta, Rothko* (La Tartaruga). Major exhibition tours from Museum Haus Lange, Krefeld to Vienna, Dortmund and Cologne (May-Dec.). Solo show at Museo Nacional, Buenos Aires (Oct.). **Demonstrations against neo-Fascists end short-lived Tambroni government. Election of John F. Kennedy as US President.**	Solo shows of *tagli* in Düsseldorf (Galerie Schmela, Jan.) and London (McRoberts & Tunnard, Oct.). Included in *Dalla natura all'arte* at Palazzo Grassi, Venice and Stedelijk Museum, Amsterdam. **Paris: *Nouveau réalisme* established. Rome: first shows of Francesco Lo Savio (Galleria Selecta) and Jannis Kounellis (La Tartaruga). Galleria Nazionale d'Arte Moderna presents Rothko retrospective (April–May). Venice: Kline wins prize.**	*Azimuth* no. 2 published at time of *La nuova concezione artistica* (New artistic conception) group show at the gallery in January. Shows *Corpi d'aria* there (May) and at Galleria Trastevere, Rome (Oct.). Solo show at Galerie Køpcke, Copenhagen (June); 7,200 metre line encased at Herning in Denmark (July). Thumb-printing and egg-eating in *Consumazione dell'arte dinamica del pubblico divorare* (Consumption of dynamic art by the devouring public), 21 July. *Achromes* made with polystyrene.
1961	Retrospective survey 1948–55 at Galleria La Medusa, Rome; show at Galerie de France, Paris. Included in *Art of Assemblage* at MOMA, New York, and *Salute to Italy*, Wadsworth Atheneum, Hartford, Connecticut. Enrico Crispolti publishes *Burri: un saggio e tre note*. **Rome: Accardi holds a solo show and Pierre Restany introduces Rotella's show of torn posters (both Galleria La Salita).**	Participates in Tokyo *Biennale* and *Salute to Italy*, Wadsworth Atheneum, Hartford, Connecticut. Periodical *Zero 3* (July) dedicated to him. Paintings for *Arte e contemplazione*, Palazzo Grassi, Venice, constitute first US solo show at Martha Jackson Gallery, New York (Nov.). Visits New York. Two solo shows in Paris (Galerie Iris Clert and Rive Droite, Nov.). **Building of Berlin Wall. USSR's Yuri Gagarin is the first man in space.**	Shows with Castellani at Galleria La Tartaruga, Rome (April). Certifies 'living sculptures'. Makes *Merda d'artista* (Artist's shit), shown in Albisola, and sealed newspaper packages. In Herning makes *Base del mondo* (Base of the world). **Milan: Umberto Eco's 'L'Informale come opera aperta' (The *informel* as an open work). *International Surrealist Exhibition* at Galleria Schwarz (May).**
1962	Buys house at Case Nove near Città di Castello. *Omaggio a Burri*, organised by Crispolti for Castello Cinquecentesco, L'Aquila. Begins *plastiche*. **New York: At Janis Gallery, De Kooning shows black and white works made in Rome. Death of Franz Kline (May).**	Exhibition at Städtisches Museum, Leverkusen (Jan.). Metal-sheet *New York* series shown in Galleria dell'Ariete, Milan (June). Second London solo show (McRoberts & Tunnard). **Paris: Death of Yves Klein (June). Venice: prizes awarded to Capogrossi and Rotella; US pavilion combines Louise Nevelson and Gorky.**	Writes *Alcune realizzazioni, Alcuni esperimenti, Alcune progetti* (Some Realisations, Some Experiments, Some Projects). Contributes to *Zero* exhibitions (Antwerp and Bern) and to *Nul* organised by the Stedelijk Museum, Amsterdam.

Year	ALBERTO BURRI	LUCIO FONTANA	PIERO MANZONI
1963	Sweeney organises retrospective for Museum of Fine Arts, Houston (Oct.–Dec.), touring in 1964. Cesare Brandi publishes monograph and catalogue for Galleria Marlborough in Rome, which travels to London (July–Aug.) and New York (1964).	*La fine di Dio* series shown at Galleria dell'Ariete, Milan (June) introduced by Dorfles; they are shown in Paris in the following year. Crispolti organises *Omaggio a Fontana* at Castello Cinquecentesco, L'Aquila (July–Oct.).	Dies 6 February in Milan.
1964	Houston retrospective tours to Buffalo, Minneapolis, San Francisco and Pasadena. Wins Premio Marzotta.	Included in *Painting & Sculpture of a Decade 54/64* at Tate Gallery, London, and in Venice Biennale and Milan *Triennale*. Begins *teatrini* series.	Galleria Schwarz holds memorial exhibition (Feb.).
1966	Room at Venice Biennale. *Fontana / Burri* exhibition organised by MOMA to travel United States, but Burri later disowns it.	Solo show at Walker Art Center, Minneapolis. Wins Gran Premio at Venice Biennale and shares *Fontana / Burri* exhibition, organised by MOMA.	
1968		Dies 7 September in Varese.	
1995	Dies 13 February in Nice.		